The Road to Educational Justice

Equitable Learning

Dr. Yashima L. Thomas-Jones

SPECIAL NOTE: To all corporations, universities, colleges, higher learning, religious and professional organizations: Quantity discounts are available on bulk purchase of this book for educational, gift purposes or as premiums for increasing magazine subscriptions or renewals. For additional information please contact www.drytj.com

Dr. Yashima L. Thomas-Jones

THIS WORK IS WRITTEN & PUBLISHED BY
Yashima L. Thomas-Jones

This is a book based on the research and thoughts of
Yashima L. Thomas-Jones

The Road to Educational Justice
Copyright© October 2024

By **Yashima L. Thomas-Jones**

Published in the United States of America by
An imprint of The LEGNA Agency LLC

www.drytj.com

Library of Congress Cataloguing-In-Publication Number
PENDING

979-8-9920189-0-5

First Edition Printing
Printed in the United States of America
October 2024

DEDICATION

To God be all the glory.

I am thankful for God's endless grace and guidance, which lightened my path.

To my nieces Eniyah and Liala, nephew Haneef, and godchildren Skylar, Mya-Ashlee, Amauri, Dontaye, and Nasir, you are the inspiration behind my passion for this work.

To all the children I had the privilege to teach, who taught me that educational justice should be the rule and not the option.

This work is a small step towards every child receiving the education they so richly deserve.

Dr. Yashima L. Thomas-Jones

Dr. Yashima L. Thomas-Jones

ACKNOWLEDGEMENTS

I thank God for allowing me to have a strong support system. Therefore, I would like to express my deepest gratitude to my mother. Her unwavering love, support, and encouragement have been a constant strength throughout my life. Your encouragement and belief in my work have carried me through to see this project through to completion. You are my forever first teacher and the captain of my cheerleading team.

To my wonderful husband, thank you for your patience, understanding, and steadfast support. You have been my rock, always reminding me of the importance of this work and inspiring me to press on.

To my amazing sister, thank you for being my confidant, cheerleader, and sounding board. Your encouragement has been invaluable.

I am deeply grateful to my extended support system, family, friends, mentors, and colleagues. You have cheered me on every step of the way. Your encouragement and faith in me have been a true gift, and I am so fortunate to have each of you in my corner.

Finally, I want to acknowledge my church family for their prayers, words of encouragement, and unwavering support. This book would not have been possible without the grace and support of the people that God has placed in my life.

Thank you all from the bottom of my heart.

What then shall we say to these things?

If God is for us, who can be against us?

Romans 8:31

Yashima

TABLE OF CONTENTS

FOREWORD

The Road to Educational Justice: Equitable Instruction invites readers to embark on a journey through time, offering a critical analysis of the historical and contemporary systems that have perpetuated educational inequities. Dr. Yashima Thomas Jones masterfully highlights the entrenched inequalities that have long served as roadblocks to educational justice, showing how deeply flawed systems and practices have led to the systematic marginalization of specific student populations, particularly African American students. These inequities are not simply the result of individual biases but are embedded within the very structures and practices of the educational system itself.

In her exploration of literacy, pedagogy, and the biases that influence academic achievement, Dr. Thomas Jones engages with a profound question that has persisted for generations: How can we claim to prepare all students for the future when the system continues to fail those who have been marginalized for centuries? Through this inquiry, she unpacks the complexities of educational inequity, illustrating how practices that are often presented as equitable in reality reinforce the very disparities they seek to dismantle.

What sets this work apart is not just its comprehensive critique but also its focus on solutions. Dr. Thomas Jones presents a compelling argument for empowering communities by redefining social justice in educational contexts. She provides a clear and actionable framework for educators, policymakers, and advocates to implement meaningful and sustainable change. Her solutions are grounded in a deep understanding of equity, inclusive pedagogy, and the transformative power of education to uplift marginalized communities.

The Road to Educational Justice challenges readers to rethink their approach to equity in education. Dr. Thomas Jones offers a comprehensive strategy for acknowledging the mistakes of the past while simultaneously charting a course for a more just future. By focusing on equitable instruction and systemic change, this work is a call for educators, leaders, and communities to unite in the fight for educational justice. It serves as both a reflection on the current state of education and a guide toward a more equitable and inclusive future, reminding us that while the journey may be long, the destination is well worth the effort.

LaShunda Reynolds, Ed.D.
Marymount University
District of Columbia Public Schools

CHAPTER 1: EQUAL, EQUITY, AND JUSTICE

Stepping into the classroom and seeing the vibrant, eager faces of the students, each carrying their own stories and aspirations. It is at this moment that educators understand the light in their students. This light reflects their potential and the necessity of advocating for educational justice. As an educator, I am personally committed to this cause, and I know that many of my colleagues share this commitment. However, some educators struggle to deliver the educational justice these children deserve. Systemic barriers and personal fears hold back many urban educators. These obstacles can significantly affect how we as educators navigate our pursuit of educational justice for our students.

The challenges are real and persistent. In the fight for educational justice, especially for African American children, debates over effective, equitable teaching practices continue even in 2024. As we engage in these debates, we watch society develop systems that undermine the strategies proven to bridge educational gaps and that support our students. The struggle for educational justice is ongoing, and we must remain vigilant. Too often, methods labeled as equity are anything but, creating further disparities and hindering the progress of African American children who desperately need and deserve authentic educational justice. For urban educators, the call is clear: we must become disruptors who rise above the challenges and commit to the methods that truly bring educational justice to our students.

I often hear administrators emphasize the importance of providing all students with equitable instruction. While this principle sounds ideal, teachers frequently express that implementing it in practice is far more challenging than it appears. The gap between theory and practice has led many educators to shy away from adopting equitable instructional practices that would foster true academic justice. As a result, minority students, particularly African American children, have faced significant academic setbacks (Aguilar, 2020; Chism, 2022; A. Evans, 2009; Howard, 2008; Lewis, 2012; Linton, 2011; Stembridge, 2020). Despite these challenges, the educational system holds the potential to achieve educational justice for African American students. To realize this potential, it is crucial that we confront and rethink the methods, materials, and cultural practices we use to educate African American children. It is not enough to simply talk about equity; we must be willing to transform our approaches to ensure that every student receives the justice they deserve in their learning experiences. By committing to these changes, we can create a more just educational landscape that truly supports African American students' academic and personal growth.

Educational justice requires us to move beyond the superficial implementation of equitable practices. Instead, educators and stakeholders should be engaging in deeper, systemic changes that dismantle the barriers African American students face. We must acknowledge how factors such as curriculum biases, limited diverse voices in educational materials, underfunded schools, and overcrowded classrooms affect the academic success of minority students. To close the academic gap, educators must commit to meaningful action that genuinely serves all students and fulfills the promise of educational justice.

The concepts of justice, equity, and equality are all seen through the same prism, and for far too long, the educational system has failed to meet the needs of the African American student population. In light of this, these three terms shouldn't be used interchangeably when discussing the education of minority students. This ongoing failure highlights the necessity of switching from equality to educational justice. When discussing equal education, we're discussing the idea that all students should have equal access to educational resources and environments, regardless of their socioeconomic background, color, gender, or aptitude. It is imperative to acknowledge that although educational equality guarantees fairness in allocating resources and prospects, it may not effectively cater to the diverse requirements of individual students. In other words, equality assumes that all children start from the same economic, social, and emotional platform. However, true equity goes beyond equality by recognizing and addressing each child's unique needs, ensuring they receive the specific support and opportunities necessary to reach their full potential. Minority students in urban school districts face various challenges, including but not limited to racial and demographic disparities, language barriers, socioeconomic status, a lack of parental support, and, in some cases, inadequate teacher preparation and poor curriculum guides. This serves as a sobering reminder that social class, race, and economic standing still predict learning results. Justice in education is therefore needed in order to impact the population of children who have received a marginalized education. Recognizing the inherent educational disparities, educational justice seeks to rectify them (Cramer et al., 2018; Datnow & Park, 2018). Educational justice is achieved when the fundamental cause of inequality is identified, and the structural barrier is removed. Consequently, no issues hinder the academic demands of African American students in the classroom because all the barriers have been addressed, and the needs of the students are being met. Therefore, the academic gap is closed, and all students excel and receive adequate opportunities.

African American Experience

In many urban areas, there is a strong prevailing sentiment that schools fail to meet the needs of African American children. Parents, educators, and some stakeholders often view educational institutions as the babysitting hub. The general feelings and thoughts are that schools offer minimal academic support and insufficient opportunities for meaningful learning and academic growth. When reflecting on both the current state of schools and the educational practices of the past, it becomes clear that little progress has been made in shifting the perception or reality of providing equitable education to African American children. Too often, African American students find themselves at the bottom of the educational hierarchy, with their needs overlooked. In some cases, migrant students and other marginalized groups receive more immediate attention and resources. This pushes African Americans further behind academically.

Therefore, the African American academic experience has had its challenges in the United States because of slavery, segregation, and systemic racism. These challenges have had long-lasting effects on educational opportunities and outcomes for African Americans. For years, African Americans have lived with the task of trying to compete in this world with sub-par education. Therefore, the pursuit of educational justice is an ongoing struggle that requires disruptors who are willing to challenge unequal systems, dismantle inequities, and create pathways that affirm the right of every African American student to a quality and empowering education.

During the era of slavery in the United States, enslaved African Americans were systemically denied access to education. Slaveholders feared that literacy and education would empower enslaved people to resist oppression and challenge the system that was created to make them feel inferior. Many slaveholders believed that African American people were inferior and undeserving of equality. Leading many White people to actively oppose educational opportunities for African Americans (Nieto, 2005). In response, laws were enacted in many southern states that made it illegal to teach enslaved individuals to read or write. Punishment for those caught defying these laws was severely punished. Ranging from physical violence to imprisonment and death.

Jefferson Davis, the first and only president of the Confederate States, exemplified racist ideologies. He believed that Black people were biologically inferior to White people. Davis asserted that black skin represents an ugly stain on the beautiful white canvas (Kendi, 2017). Davis's views were not isolated. They reflected and reinforced societal beliefs that justified the suppression of education as a means to maintain racial hierarchy and economic control over a marginalized group of people. Despite the risks of these oppressive laws and beliefs, enslaved African Americans demonstrated extraordinary resilience in their pursuit of knowledge.

In many cases, enslaved African Americans risked severe punishment to learn to read and write. The enslaved organized secret schools where they gathered in woods, churches, or abandoned buildings to receive lessons from literate members of their community, sympathetic Whites, abolitionists, and Northern missionaries. They used the Bible as a tool for learning. African Americans' determination to learn and be literate never wavered (Darling-Hammond, 2006). These educational efforts were courageous but remained sporadic and dangerous due to the systemic barriers. It made it nearly impossible to establish widespread literacy among enslaved African Americans. The legacy of these laws and the systematic exclusion of African Americans from education have had a lasting impact. It set the stage for the deep educational inequalities that persist today.

The struggle for educational justice did not end with the abolition of slavery. Many believed that education was essential for newly freed African Americans after the Civil War. The Freedman's Bureau established schools across the South to address this need. These schools include Penn School in South Carolina, The Storer College of West Virginia, and approximately 66 schools in Texas. They became hubs for African American learning. The Bureau did not integrate schools. Instead, they created separate institutions that, despite their value, lack of funding, and qualified teachers, still taught over 20,000 African Americans to be literate (Davis, 2017; Hornsby, 1973; Price, 2018). The reality of the Freedman Bureau schools remained inequitable, proving that African Americans received inferior education opportunities. It reinforced the racial educational divide.

The Freedman's Bureau's efforts were limited by scarce resources and deeply entrenched racism. Schools faced threats and violent backlash from the Klu Klux Klan and other groups that opposed African American advancement. Federal funding stifled the Bureau's progress in its mission to provide equitable education. By 1872, the Freedman's Bureau was dismantled. This left African American families seeking quality education on their own through grassroots efforts to build community-run schools. The challenges of this era laid the groundwork for the ongoing struggle for educational equity. This structure revealed how systemic barriers to quality education were initially structured.

This historical context remains relevant today. The legacy of the Freedman's Bureau era persists in current disparities in school funding, access to qualified teachers, and academic resources that predominately affect African Americans and other marginalized communities. Today, activists, policymakers, and educators are still working to dismantle these systemic barriers that trace back to post-Civil War policies and beliefs. The efforts to secure equitable funding, diverse curriculum, and supportive school environments underscore a commitment to rectify past inequalities, ensuring that all students, regardless of race, have access to a high-quality education. Continued advocacy should reflect the deep roots of educational justice as a movement born from historical struggles. There is an attempt to redefine the challenges to meet a modern educational landscape.

During this period, historically black colleges and universities (HBCUs) were established, often by religious organizations and abolitionists, to provide higher education to African Americans. The HBCUs, Mary McLeod Bethune, and other notable African Americans advocated for equality and educational equity for minority students (Muhammad et al., 2020). They did not rely solely on the Freedman Bureau to create equitable practices for African American students. They created an educational environment where African American students excel (Muhammad et al., 2020). The efforts of the community impacted African American students, yielding equitable results. However, the general population of African Americans had limited access to the educational foundation offered. Therefore, the educational gap of this broader population of underserved students continued to widen (A. Evans, 2009). Many of the HBCUs were plagued with financial issues and faced fierce resistance from white supremacists. Schools for African Americans were often targets of violence, including arson and attacks by groups like the Ku Klux Klan. This violence was intended to intimidate African Americans and prevent them from pursuing education (Colby, 1985; Kendi, 2017; Muhammad et al., 2020; Rucker & Jubilee, 2007). By understanding the historical denial of education and the courageous efforts made by African Americans to gain literacy, we can better appreciate the ongoing journey toward educational justice (Muhammad et al., 2020). This history underscores the importance of addressing the legacy of exclusion and working towards an equitable future for all children, regardless of race, ethnicity, or socioeconomic status.

Following the end of Reconstruction, Southern states implemented Jim Crow laws. This mandated racial segregation in all public facilities, including schools. The landmark Supreme Court decision in Plessy v. Ferguson upheld the separate but equal doctrines. This ruling meant that African American schools were vastly inferior to those for white students. As time progressed, many White people continued to view African Americans as inferior and undeserving of equality and equity in education. The thought was that African Americans acted like animals and lived to satisfy their wants (Kendi, 2017; Nieto, 2005). The idea of inferiority and oppositional culture existed for years and established the framework for the instruction of African American children. Society has unequivocally sent the message that African Americans are regarded as individuals of no value and are not encouraged to strive for greatness, but rather accept a state of mediocrity (Baldwin, 1963/1988). Throughout generations, African Americans have endeavored to disprove the fallacy surrounding their aptitude to acquire knowledge and excel in society. Attempting daily to dismantle the idea that African American people adhere to detrimental societal norms that hinder academic success, leading to their lower accomplishments compared to White and Asian students (Lewis, 2012). Therefore, African American students are subjected to institutional racism in the educational system. These students contend with receiving an unfair education (Kendi, 2017; Linton, 2011; Stembridge, 2020).

African American schools were chronically underfunded, with fewer resources, poorly paid teachers, and inadequate facilities. Many schools lacked basic supplies, textbooks, and proper buildings, severely limiting the quality of education African American children received. The underfunding of schools has a deep and lasting impact on educational justice. Addressing these issues requires more than just equal but equitable funding. The funding gaps can have long-term effects on students' academic success. Acknowledging and addressing the historical and systemic funding discrepancies can change African American students' trajectory. However, Schools in African American neighborhoods remained underfunded and underserved, perpetuating the cycle of educational inequality.

African American students have varying educational experiences and have different experiences upon leaving school (Ainscow, 2012). Lawrence (2005) and Barnes (2021) also stated that Black students have traditionally been deprived of equitable educational chances and resources that are accessible to their White peers. The U.S. educational system has undergone many changes over the years.

Nevertheless, the results for African American children continue to be quite disappointing. Hence, the involvement of the family can either contribute to or hinder the achievement of educational equity. As stated by Lareau (2011), parents' social status significantly influences children's academic experience. This is because it leads families to have different perspectives on education, which in turn affects the equitable treatment they receive in their educational journey. Lareau argued that children raised in middle-class households acquire a sense of entitlement due to their ability to interact with adults on an equal footing, a phenomenon she referred to as "concerted cultivation" (p. 2). Thus, engaging with principals and teachers enables these children and parents to proficiently advocate for equitable treatment and impartiality (Lareau, 2011).

As a result, children from disadvantaged socioeconomic situations do not have an equal educational experience due to instances where their families feel intimidated by the educational experts they interact with. The family believes that teachers are the main providers of instruction for children. These parents establish distinct boundaries between adults and children and prohibit youngsters from advocating for themselves. The justification is that children should remain in their designated role as children (Lareau, 2011). There is also an underlying fear of educational leaders because these parents lack the confidence and vocabulary to articulate their exact thoughts regarding their children's education (Lareau, 2011). Furthermore, Lareau found that these parents consider education to be the responsibility of educators. So, they anticipate that teachers and school personnel will bear the primary responsibility for making certain their children receive all the knowledge they should.

This contrast between the socio-economic status of parents and educational leaders strongly impacts the dynamics of teaching and learning in the school setting (Lareau, 2011).

Linton (2011) had similar views on the influence of social class on education and social standing. A significant number of White Americans struggle to grasp the importance of comprehending equitable treatment and diversity and its relevance. As a result, numerous individuals of Caucasian descent associate with the idea that there exists a sense of liberation associated with being White, which grants them effortless entry into scholastic achievements.

In order to attain meaningful educational equity, it is crucial to use instructional methodologies that acknowledge and tackle the distinct obstacles African American children encounter. Equitable instructional methods extend beyond just offering identical resources or curriculum to all students; they encompass a deliberate endeavor to customize education to meet students at their current level and address their unique needs. In order to establish an educational setting in which African American children are valued and understood, it is imperative to incorporate culturally relevant instruction. This approach incorporates African American children's cultural backgrounds, experiences, and history into the curriculum. By employing this approach, educators enhance the learning experience's relevance and validate African American students' identities (Lazaro, 2006; Sandoval et al., 2011).

Despite the historical biases that have often led to lower expectations for African American students, research consistently shows that high expectations are crucial for academic success. Even after the integration of schools,

21

African American students continue to face implicit biases and discriminatory practices that hinder their educational experiences.

To improve this broken system of equitable education, educators need professional development to recognize and address their biases. Schools must also implement policies that promote equity in areas such as discipline, special education placement, and access to extracurricular opportunities. Equitable instructional practices involve challenging African American students with a rigorous curriculum that prepares them for college and careers while providing the necessary support to help them meet those high expectations. This can include access to advanced coursework, mentorship programs, and resources that foster academic growth. According to Linton (2011), many African American students suffer unfair outcomes from an equal approach to education, which can have a significant negative influence on their personal and academic lives. As a result, teachers need to provide this marginalized group of students with educational justice. In the urban school districts of the United States, the issue of equity impacts a large number of African American children (Darling-Hammond, 2006).

African American Vernacular English

Many people frown upon how most African Americans speak, leading many to believe that most African Americans are uneducated because they do not navigate the English language properly. Therefore, African American people were labeled ignorant or unintelligent. This would lead to many African American children participating in speech programs at school or receiving an inadequate education compared to their peers. Most Americans were unaware that African Americans speak a dialect of English with its own grammatical structure, usage, and pronunciation rules, according to speech pathologist Shontaye Jones. Therefore, many African Americans are considered to use African American Vernacular English (AAVE), and the dialect varies according to geographic region with fluctuating dialects (Johnson et al., 2023). This has a major impact on their academics and obtaining educational justice.

As time progressed, African American Vernacular English (AAVE) was identified as a dialect many African American people spoke. This dialect is also known as Ebonics, but it is a cross between African languages and nonstandard colonial English. The dialect was developed by enslaved African Americans to cope with slavery and depression as they endured that difficult time (Filmer, 2003). Therefore, AAVE has the ability to convey an extensive range of culture through various forms like blues, gospel, R&B, Motown, sounding, the dozens, hip-hop, drama, poetry, prose, oratory, scholarship, satire, oral narrative, and more (Filmer, 2003). AAVE significantly impacts educational justice for African American children, primarily through the ways it is perceived and treated within the educational system. Speech is an indisputable measure of social standing, a definitive sign of belonging to any specific group (Filmer, 2003).

Many teachers and educational systems hold biases against AAVE, viewing it as "incorrect" or "uneducated" language. This bias can result in lower expectations for students who use AAVE. This can negatively impact African American student's academic opportunities and outcomes. This type of discrimination contributes to the systemic marginalization of African American students, perpetuating educational inequities. For many African American children, AAVE is part of their cultural identity. When schools dismiss or devalue AAVE, they undermine these students' cultural heritage, leading to feelings of alienation and diminished self-worth (Filmer, 2008; Fisher & Tapp, 2013; Harris & Schfoeder, 2013; Johnson et al., 2023; Snow, 2019).

Therefore, African American children are often expected to "code-switch" between AAVE and Standard American English in the academic setting. The pressure for students to code-switch places additional emotional and cognitive burdens on those who are often marginalized academically. Recognizing and incorporating African American students' home language and culture is important to affirm their identity and promote a sense of belonging. This led to legal cases and policies surrounding the recognition of AAVE. In most schools, there was a lack of respect for integrating diverse linguistics that helped develop a strong, positive identity in language for African American children. Therefore, in 1996, an Oakland Ebonics Resolution was instituted. It highlighted the need for educational policies that respected linguistic diversity and supported the educational needs of African American children (Filmer, 2003). However, the lack of widespread policy implementation throughout the country continues to perpetuate educational inequities.

According to notable subject matter experts (Filmer, 2008; Fisher & Tapp, 2013; Harris & Schfoeder, 2013; Johnson et al., 2023; Snow, 2019), they indicate that when the curriculum fails to reflect students' linguistic diversity, it can hinder comprehension, participation, and learning. This leads to a disconnect between the student's home language and the language of instruction. Therefore, it reinforces the notion that their home language is inferior, contributing to internalized racism and educational disengagement. Furthermore, school assessments do not take into consideration that many African American students use AAVE, knowing that assessments use Standard American English. The misalignment often results in lower test scores. This is not because of the student's intelligence or knowledge but because the tests do not accurately reflect the language, they use to express their knowledge. Therefore, the test scores misrepresent the academic potential of African American students. This leads to unfair tracking and placement decisions for this group of students.

The impact of AAVE on educational justice for African American children is profound. How schools and educators respond to AAVE can contribute to or mitigate the educational inequities that African American students face. Therefore, embracing linguistic diversity and addressing biases against AAVE are essential to achieving educational justice.

Brown v. Board of Education

The 1954 landmark Supreme Court case Brown v. Board of Education marked a turning point in the fight for civil rights. The court declared that state laws establishing separate public schools for African American students were unconstitutional. This decision not only dismantled the legal foundation of racial segregation in education but also rejected the deeply ingrained notion that separate could ever be equal. By overturning the Plessy v. Ferguson ruling and its 'separate but equal' doctrine, Brown established that equitable educational opportunities were a fundamental right for all students, regardless of race. This ruling laid the groundwork for desegregation, opening the door to more just and inclusive educational environments. Yet, while Brown was monumental in theory, its promise of true equity in education remains a challenge in practice. Achieving genuine educational justice remains an ongoing commitment to dismantling the systemic barriers that continue to impact African American students and other marginalized communities today.

Despite the ruling, many Southern states resisted desegregation. In some areas, schools were closed rather than integrated. African American students faced hostility, violence, and harassment when attempting to attend all-white schools. The federal government often had to intervene to enforce desegregation orders. Many African American students continued to face de facto segregation due to residential and economic disparities.

Brown v. Board of Education challenged systemic bias embedded in educational institutions. It also raised questions about the resources essential for equitable learning environments. While the verdict was instrumental in dismantling explicit racial segregation, it lacked actionable guidelines or standards to ensure fair and equitable educational opportunities for African American students. Although *Brown* recognized that segregated schools fostered inequality, stigmas, and inferiority. It did not provide a roadmap to counteract these disadvantages. The ruling's failure to address the practical aspects of educational equity, as cycles of disadvantage rooted in the past continue to shape the educational experiences of marginalized African American communities today.

Many African American students are still more likely to attend schools that are underfunded, under-resourced, and segregated in practice. This reality underscores the need to focus on desegregation and equitable instructional practices that address the specific needs of African American students within the educational system. According to Barth (2016), there has been a concerning trend of schools becoming segregated again based on race and poverty despite previous efforts to integrate them. This suggests that ongoing structural and societal challenges are preventing African American students from receiving a high-quality public education on an equal basis.

According to Stembridge (2020), the current situation maintains the existing state of affairs, which is characterized by the historical connections between racism, economic circumstances, and political marginalization. These factors contribute to certain groups being more susceptible to underperforming in school compared to others. Stembridge indicates that Black and Latinx children face a higher frequency of disciplinary measures, are not adequately represented in gifted and talented programs, and are more likely to be instructed by less competent teachers at schools that are both high-poverty and segregated. Consequently, schools were not specifically created to ensure equal opportunities for all children. Educational access and equity were only provided to White males because they were expected to succeed and had a sense of entitlement.

The decision in *Brown v. Board of Education* was a crucial victory in the fight for civil rights, but the work of achieving educational equity for African American students continues. Equitable instructional practices are essential to fulfilling *Brown's* promise, ensuring that African American students not only share the same classrooms as their peers but also receive the quality education they deserve. Reflecting on *Brown*, educators must commit to creating educational environments where African American students can thrive and achieve the academic success and personal growth envisioned by those who fought for their right to an equal education.

Federal Educational Mandates

Our educational system continues to look for ways to bridge the educational gap and provide equity for African American children. The U.S. federal government implemented policies that attempted to bridge the educational gap for minority students, such as No Child Left Behind (NCLB), The Every Child Succeeds Act (ECSA), and the Individuals with Disabilities Education Act (IDEA). However, enacting these policies has yet to close the educational gap and has caused significant frustration among all educational stakeholders.

Former President George W. Bush implemented No Child Left Behind (NCLB) in 2002. The overall premise of this federal educational mandate was to close the academic gap and focus on equality. The components of NCLB are intended to ensure that every child can learn and is expected to learn in schools by delegating responsibility for students' success or failure to educators (Chu, 2019). This mandate frustrated educators because they carried the heavy burden of educating students with limited support and resources from administrators.

NCLB increased accountability, required states to test students in reading and math annually, and reported the results by subgroups. This transparency was intended to spotlight achievement gaps and pressure schools to address them (Chu, 2019). There was a focus on low-performing schools. Many schools that consistently underperformed served a large population of African American students. These schools faced sanctions and were required to implement improvement plans (Evans, 2009). The intention was to ensure that schools could not ignore the needs of African American students. Therefore, NCLB emphasized the importance of having "highly qualified "teachers in schools serving disadvantaged students. This was to ensure that African American students had access to effective educators.

Despite its intentions, NCLB faced significant criticism, particularly regarding its impact on African American students. The high-stakes testing led many schools to focus on test preparation at the expense of not providing equity to a vulnerable population of students, which often limited the educational experience of African American students (Chu, 2019; Evans, 2009). The policy came with resource disparities that did not sufficiently address the underlying inequities that many predominantly African American schools faced. Without proper funding and support, many schools could not meet the demands of NCLB, exacerbating the challenges facing African American students (Chu, 2019). Lastly, school sanctions had an impact on equitable practices for African American students. This led to instability in schools serving African American communities. This instability further disadvantage students, frequent changes in leadership or teaching staff disrupted the learning environment.

As I explored the connections between NCLB and equity for African American students, it's important to recognize that while it had the potential to advance educational equity, its implementation often fell short of addressing the systemic barriers faced by African American students (Chu, 2019; Evans, 2009). The focus on accountability and data transparency was a step toward equity, but the lack of support for addressing deeper inequalities limited its effectiveness. NCLB serves as a critical case study for understanding the complexities of education reform and its impact on marginalized communities.

The Every Student Succeeds Act (ESSA) of 2015 is a pivotal piece of legislation with significant implications for equitable education, particularly for African American students (Evans, 2009). ESSA has the promise and challenges of addressing long-standing educational disparities. It was designed to replace the No Child Left Behind Act (NCLB), which had garnered criticism for its heavy emphasis on standardized testing and its one-size-fits-all approach to accountability (Chu, 2019; Evans, 2009). ESSA sought to correct these issues by granting states more flexibility in assessing and improving school performance. At its core, ESSA emphasizes the need for equity, particularly for historically marginalized groups, including African American students.

This new educational initiative was designed to positively impact equitable education. ESSA targeted support for low-performing schools and increased accountability for all subgroups. This act also provided support for culturally relevant pedagogy. In theory, the goals of ESSA would provide African American students with educational justice.

ESSA required states to identify and provide support the lowest performing 5% of schools and high schools with graduation rates below 67%. Since a disproportionate number of African American students attend underperforming schools, this provision holds the potential to direct much-needed resources and interventions to these schools, thereby addressing systemic inequities (Chu, 2019; Evans, 2009). Because ESSA gives states considerable discretion in how they meet its requirements, the degree to which African American students benefit can vary widely from state to state. Some states may prioritize equity more than others, leading to inconsistencies in the resources and support that African American students receive.

According to ESSA, states are required to report data not just on overall student performance but also on the performance of specific subgroups, including African American students. This transparency ensures that disparities in educational outcomes cannot be overlooked or masked by overall school performance. By holding schools accountable for the success of every subgroup, ESSA pushes for more tailored strategies to meet the needs of African American students. While ESSA identifies low-performing schools for additional support, the law does not guarantee that all schools will receive the necessary funding to address the disparities (Chu, 2019; Evans, 2009). Schools in predominantly African American communities often face chronic underfunding, which can limit the effectiveness of the interventions proposed under ESSA.

ESSA encourages states and districts to implement evidence-based interventions, which can include culturally relevant teaching practices. These practices are crucial for African American students, as they help to create a more inclusive and affirming educational environment that acknowledges and values their cultural backgrounds, leading to better engagement and academic outcomes. Despite the law's intentions, African American students continue to face challenges such as racial bias in discipline, lower expectations from educators, and less access to advanced coursework (Chu, 2019; Evans, 2009). ESSA alone cannot solve these deep-seated issues; it requires a concerted effort from educators, policymakers, and communities to dismantle these barriers.

The Every Student Succeeds Act has the potential to significantly impact equitable education for African American students by promoting accountability, supporting underperforming schools, and encouraging culturally relevant teaching (Chu, 2019; Evans, 2009). However, its success in achieving true equity is contingent on the commitment and actions of states and local districts. It's crucial to identify

ESSA's promise and the ongoing challenges that must be addressed to ensure that African American students receive the high-quality, equitable education they deserve.

The Individuals with Disabilities Education Act (IDEA) is a federal law that ensures students with disabilities receive a free and appropriate public education (FAPE) tailored to their individual needs. While IDEA has been instrumental in providing necessary services and accommodations to students with disabilities, there are critical concerns regarding its implementation, especially when it comes to African American students. One of the significant issues under IDEA is the disproportionality of African American students being identified as having disabilities, particularly in categories like emotional disturbance and intellectual disabilities. This overrepresentation can often result from implicit biases, cultural misunderstandings, and systemic inequities in the education system. African American students are more likely to be placed in restrictive environments and are often subject to harsher disciplinary actions, which can exacerbate educational inequities.

To address these educational disparities, equitable instructional practices that recognize and value African American students' cultural and linguistic diversity are crucial. Educators must be trained to understand and incorporate students' cultural backgrounds into their teaching practices. This helps create a more inclusive classroom environment where African American students feel seen and respected. Ongoing professional development to address implicit biases is essential. Educators need to be aware of how their perceptions of race and disability might affect their teaching and decision-making processes.

Engaging with families and communities in meaningful ways can provide educators with deeper insights into the students' backgrounds, strengths, and needs. This collaboration ensures that instructional strategies are more aligned with the students' real-life experiences. Instruction should be tailored to meet the diverse needs of students. Differentiated instruction allows for multiple ways of teaching and assessing students, which can be particularly beneficial for those who have been mislabeled or underserved.

There is a growing recognition that IDEA needs to be reformed to better address the needs of African American students. Ensuring that the assessment and identification processes for disabilities are culturally and linguistically appropriate, reducing the risk of misidentification. Schools and districts should be held accountable for disproportionality in special education. This includes transparent data reporting and interventions when disparities are identified. Providing educators with the resources, training, and support they need to implement equitable practices is crucial for the success of all students.

The intersection of IDEA, African American students, and equitable instructional practices highlights the need for ongoing efforts to ensure that all students receive the education they deserve. Addressing the disproportionality and ensuring that instructional practices are equitable and inclusive will require a systemic change, involving educators, policymakers, families, and communities working together.

Missionary Syndrome

Missionary syndrome refers to the mindset in which educators, often from privileged backgrounds, approach teaching African American students with a savior complex (Linton, 2011). This perspective can significantly impact educational justice in several ways because these educators have low expectations and deficit thinking. In most cases, they are culturally insensitive and reinforce stereotypes. Therefore, illuminating inequitable education for African American students.

Educators with a missionary mindset may view African American students as inherently disadvantaged and in need of "saving." This can lead to lowered expectations, where teachers don't challenge students academically, believing they are incapable of higher achievement. This undermines educational equity by denying students the opportunity to reach their full potential. This type of educator, impose their own cultural values and norms, disregarding the rich cultural heritage and experiences of African American students. This can create an educational environment that feels alienating and unwelcoming, further marginalizing students.

The missionary mindset often involves making decisions for students without involving them or their communities in the process. This approach strips students of their efficacy, reinforcing power imbalances and perpetuating systemic inequities in education. By assuming that African American students need "saving," educators may unconsciously reinforce harmful stereotypes about race and ability. This not only affects how students see themselves but also how others perceive them in the educational system. Educators with a missionary mindset may focus on individual students' perceived deficiencies rather than addressing the broader systemic issues that create and perpetuate educational inequities. This can divert attention away from necessary structural changes, such as curriculum reform, resource allocation, and policy advocacy.

Overall, missionary syndrome can perpetuate educational injustice by maintaining and reinforcing the very inequities it seeks to address. For African American students, this means continued marginalization, reduced opportunities, and a failure to recognize and nurture their inherent strengths and potential.

Educational Justice

Obtaining educational justice for African American students is imperative for several reasons, all of which are deeply rooted in the principles of equity, fairness, and social justice. Addressing historical inequalities is critical to achieving educational justice for African American students. African American students have historically been subjected to systemic racism and discrimination, both within and outside the educational system. From the era of slavery to the Jim Crow laws and beyond, African Americans have been denied equal access to quality education (Kendi, 2017). These historical injustices have created generational disadvantages, and achieving educational justice is crucial in addressing these long-standing inequities.

African American students often face an achievement gap compared to their peers, which is largely due to disparities in resources, access to high-quality teachers, and biases in the educational system. Educational justice seeks to close this gap by ensuring African American students have the same opportunities to succeed academically as any other student, improving their life chances and socio-economic mobility (Thomas-Jones, 2024). When African American students receive a high-quality education, they are more likely to access higher education opportunities, secure better-paying jobs, and contribute positively to society. Educational justice helps break the cycle of poverty and opens doors for future generations to achieve economic stability and success.

Ensuring educational equity is a crucial element in the wider struggle against institutional racism. Schools and educational institutions have a substantial impact on either maintaining or questioning societal inequalities. By ensuring that African American students receive equitable treatment and equal opportunity, educational systems may confront and destroy the systems that support and maintain racial prejudice. Ensuring educational equity for African American children is not solely focused on individual gains, but rather on fostering a just and inclusive society. Society reaps the benefits of a more varied, knowledgeable, and involved population when every student, regardless of their race, have equal access to high-quality education. This fosters social unity, mitigates social conflicts, and cultivates a culture of inclusivity and mutual regard.

Education is a powerful tool for empowerment. By ensuring educational justice, African American communities are empowered to advocate for themselves, address community challenges, and build collective strength. This empowerment extends beyond the classroom and has the potential to transform entire communities. Finally, achieving educational justice for African American students is moral and ethical. It is about upholding the fundamental principles of human rights and dignity. Every child, regardless of their background, has the right to a quality education. Denying this right to African American students is not only unjust but also undermines the values of equality and fairness that are foundational to a democratic society.

Culturally relevant teaching (CRT) is essential in creating educational justice. A classroom environment where

36

African American students feel valued and understood allows for equitable practices. This approach involves integrating African American students' cultural backgrounds, experiences, and histories into the curriculum. It also addresses historical and systemic inequities in education. When educators make learning more relatable and affirm African American students' identities it builds a trusting relationship where students feel safe, respected, and willing to take academic risks. CRT helps to counteract the legacy of exclusion and marginalization that Brown v Board of Education sought to overturn.

Educational justice for African American students is crucial not only for their individual success but also for the health and future of society as a whole. It addresses deep-rooted historical wrongs, closes achievement gaps, promotes social mobility, and challenges systemic racism. By achieving educational justice, we move closer to a society where all individuals are valued, respected, and given the opportunity to reach their full potential.

No Educational Justice, No Educational Peace
The pursuit of educational justice is not merely a moral imperative, it is a necessary foundation for true educational peace. There is a distinction between equality, equity, and justice for African American children in urban schools. It just does not impact the students' academics. They have lived realities that shape their experiences and future. The principle of equality provides the same resources and opportunities to all students. It overlooks the systemic inequities that have historically marginalized and disadvantaged African American children. Equality alone cannot rectify these entrenched disparities because it assumes a level playing field that does not exist. Equity, in contrast, recognizes these

structural barriers. It calls for the allocation of resources and support in a way that addresses these specific challenges. Yet, even equity falls short without the larger context of justice. There is a need to dismantle the very systems and practices that perpetuate racial inequities in the first place.

Justice seeks to eliminate the root of educational oppression. It ensures that every African American child not only has what they need to succeed. They would thrive in an environment that honors their culture. Without educational justice, there can be no educational peace. African American Children in urban schools continue to feel the weight of systemic discrimination and diminished expectations. Justice is significant because it moves beyond superficial solutions. It requires immediate results that support educational justice. It insists on transformative changes. Those changes should involve revisiting and revising policies, practices, and mindsets that have denied African American children the education they deserve.

When we advocate for educational justice, we are requiring society to acknowledge the historical wrongs that created the educational divide. While actively working to right the wrongs. In our advocation, we desire that the educational system see African American children not just as students but as powerful individuals capable of their own destinies. Only through educational justice can we create an educational landscape that is truly equitable. African American children should have the space and support to reach their fullest potential. Until justice is achieved, educational peace remains elusive, and the struggle for educational justice will continue to be an urgent cause.

CHAPTER 2: EARLY EDUCATION

Historically, many African American families relied on family members, or the community members known as the village, to provide childcare for their preschool-age children. This stemmed from the common belief that formal learning began in kindergarten. As a result, many young children spent their primary years with relatives or trusted neighbors, receiving valuable emotional support and supervision. This was a familiar and safe environment for them and their parents. These informal settings offered benefits, such as reduced exposure to accidents and a nurturing atmosphere. However, they often lacked structure or academically focused activities that could stimulate early cognitive development. This inadvertently contributed to the educational gap that emerged even before children entered kindergarten (Iruka, 2022).

For African American students, early education is crucial in shaping educational justice. It can reinforce or challenge systemic inequities. Research demonstrates that early education programs are foundational in developing children's cognitive, social, and emotional skills (Barnett et al., 2013; Iruka, 2022; Jarrett & Coba-Rodriguez, 2018). Yet for many African American children, access to academically enriching programs remains limited, which poses challenges to achieving equitable educational outcomes and reinforces systemic disparities in the educational system. The lack of access to quality early education often results in children entering formal schooling already at a disadvantage. This widens the academic achievement gap and affects their long-term educational trajectory. Addressing these disparities through expanding access to high-quality early childhood programs is essential for advancing educational justice. This ensures that all children have a fair academic start regardless of background.

Foundation for Learning

Early education sets the foundation for lifelong learning. African American students who received high-quality early education are more likely to develop strong academic skills. This early academic success can reduce achievement gaps that often widen as students progress through the educational system (Barnett et al., 2013). Before entering kindergarten, African American children who do not have their educational needs adequately met in their first five years of life face academic deficits (Barnett et al., 2013). A child's early years are critical for cognitive development and emotional and social development. Therefore, the failure to meet the needs of African American students during this period can have profound and lasting effects on the academic trajectory and overall life outcomes. This impacts individual children and has broader implications for educational justice and equity.

The early years of a child's life are a critical development window. This Is when children experience rapid brain development and form foundational cognitive skills like language, numeracy, and problem-solving abilities (Barnett et al., 2013). If African American students do not receive adequate educational stimulation during this time, they will likely enter school at a disadvantage. This lack of preparedness can lead to struggles with adjusting to school routines, following instructions, and engaging with curriculum content. They will also lack the basic skills critical for academic success and be placed in a vulnerable position of not receiving educational justice.

When African American children do not have their academic needs met in the first five years, it sets the stage for a range of academic, emotional, and social challenges that can persist throughout their lives. This hinders their potential and exacerbates systemic inequities, making the fight for educational justice more difficult. Addressing these early needs is therefore crucial for ensuring that African American children have the opportunity to succeed academically and contribute fully to society.

In search of a solution to fix the broken educational system for African American children, Head Start was established by former President Lyndon B. Johnson in 1965. It addressed the necessity of enhancing and narrowing educational inequity. This program specifically targeted the educational and developmental requirements of children belonging to low-income families, particularly those residing in African American areas. The program offered comprehensive early childhood education, health, nutrition, and parental engagement for children and their families (Iruka, 2022).

In the early 1960s, African American communities faced significant educational disparities. There was systemic racism, segregation, and economic inequality that plagued the community, and there was not much hope in sight. Head Start was designed to provide access to early childhood education. This was often unavailable or of poor quality in African American children's neighborhoods. The goal was to give this group of students a strong start in their educational journey. This would help bridge the gap in school readiness between them and their more affluent peers.

At its inception, Head Start challenged segregation and discrimination in education. The support of this federal

41

program helped counteract the effects of systemic racism and promote greater equity in educational opportunities. This was the main desire of many African American families who wanted their children to experience an equitable early childhood educational experience.

Although programs such as Head Start have been instrumental in delivering early childhood education to disadvantaged communities and offering comprehensive education, health, and nutrition services to African American children, there is still an ongoing need to tackle wider systemic inequalities that impact educational achievements. The White House Initiative on Educational Excellence for African Americans is crucial in this context. The Initiative not only addresses the early learning needs of African American children but also aims to eliminate the longstanding obstacles that impede their educational achievement throughout their academic path, distinguishing it from traditional early education programs. The Initiative seeks to establish an educational environment that fosters the success of African American children, from early childhood education to college, through its emphasis on policy advocacy, community participation, and resource allocation.

Therefore, in 2012, under the leadership of former President Obama, the White House implemented an Initiative on Educational Excellence with a specific focus on improving educational outcomes for African Americans. This program, similar to Head Start, has a significant impact on shaping early childhood education and advancing equitable educational opportunities for African American children (Barrett et al., 2018). The project highlights the significance of early childhood education as a fundamental basis for continuous learning throughout one's life. It promotes the expansion of high-quality early learning programs, which are essential for African American children who are disproportionately impacted by inadequate access and resources. This emphasis aids in equalizing opportunities by ensuring that African American children are prepared to study when they attend school, thereby diminishing disparities in academic performance right from the beginning.

The initiative emphasizes the significance of culturally responsive teaching and the necessity for early development programs that acknowledge and assist African American children's distinct cultural and linguistic needs. This strategy promotes the development of a favorable self-concept and cultivates a supportive educational environment that can alleviate the adverse impacts of systemic bias. The effort has actively advocated for measures that advance educational justice, including endorsing programs focusing on early childhood education. It aims to minimize systemic obstacles that impede educational opportunities for African American children, including those in early education environments, by influencing federal and state policy. One aspect of the initiative's efforts includes campaigning for equitable distribution of resources to schools and early development programs that cater to African American populations. This encompasses the allocation of financial resources for the construction and maintenance of buildings, procurement of instructional resources, and training programs for teachers, all of which are crucial for delivering a superior educational experience.

The effort prioritizes actively involving African American parents and communities in education. It aims to empower parents with the necessary knowledge and resources to effectively advocate for their children, ensuring that African

American children receive support from their families and educational institutions. Fostering collaboration among schools, community organizations, and other stakeholders to establish nurturing settings for African American children. These partnerships are crucial for tackling the wider societal factors influencing educational achievement, such as healthcare, housing, and financial security. The initiative assists in research and data collection endeavors that emphasize the discrepancies in early childhood education for African American children. This data is utilized to shape policies and strategies that advocate for educational equity, guaranteeing that actions are focused and efficient. The effort aims to develop and promote effective methods in early childhood education, with the goal of sharing successful models that may be duplicated in other communities. This will have a wider impact on achieving educational justice.

By addressing early childhood education, these initiatives aim to break the cycle that many African American children face. Early intervention is critical in preventing the cumulative effects of educational disparities, which can persist throughout a child's academic journey and into adulthood. Ensuring that African American children receive a strong start in early childhood education is a fundamental step toward achieving educational justice. It helps to build a foundation for academic success, higher graduation rates, and better opportunities for higher education and employment. The White House Initiative on Educational Excellence for African Americans significantly impacts early childhood learning by promoting access to quality education, advocating for equitable policies, engaging families and communities, and supporting research that drives educational justice. By focusing on these areas, the initiative contributes to reducing disparities and ensuring that African American children have the opportunity to thrive from their earliest years.

Addressing Systemic Inequities in Early Childhood

As an educator, I have observed how inequalities in education have a significant and enduring effect on educational equity, especially for African American children. These disparities frequently become apparent in early childhood education. The imbalances manifest in schools that lack sufficient resources, curriculum that exhibit bias, discriminatory disciplinary methods, disparities in health, and inadequate parental support and involvement.

Years following the Brown v. Board of Education case, numerous African American children still reside in disadvantaged communities with limited access to high-quality early education. The absence of opportunities to attend high-quality preschools, early learning centers, and other essential educational facilities results in notable disparities in preparedness for school as compared to peers who have had more comprehensive early educational experiences. A significant number of educational institutions that African American students attend do not adequately fulfill their fundamental educational requirements. Instead of participating in serious academic teaching, they partake in meaningless recreation. The students experience this due to socioeconomic differences, school funding, and societal expectations.

There are families who seek to enroll their children in a preschool program that provides support and enriching opportunities. However, schools in predominantly African American communities are often underfunded, leading to larger class sizes, fewer resources, and less access to enrichment programs. Furthermore, the parents cannot financially afford early childhood schools. The lack of parental financial abilities and underfunding of state and federal government investment in early childhood education perpetuates a cycle of inequitable education. These social disparities significantly impact early childhood development because there is a struggle to provide children with books, educational toys, and enriching experiences, making it difficult for children to achieve their overall potential.

African American children who are given the chance to participate in early childhood programs encounter a widespread type of racism that affects how they are treated in the early educational environment. Unconscious biases can result in reduced expectations, unfairly singling out disciplinary problems or learning difficulties, and limiting possibilities for advanced learning (Rashid, 2009). There are some early childhood facilities where certain instructors exhibit microaggressions, resulting in more severe consequences for children of color in comparison to their white counterparts. Research has indicated that African American students have a higher likelihood of facing suspension or expulsion for acts that are frequently disregarded among white youngsters. This contributes to the school-to-prison pipeline, wherein early disciplinary encounters in educational institutions increase the probability of being incarcerated in the future and impact the educational instruction of the children (Berry, 2023; Iruka, 2022; Rashid, 2009).

Educators desire to have great connections with home and school. However, systemic barriers can affect how schools engage with African American families. Stereotypes and biases result in the notion that African American parents have lower levels of involvement in their children's education, which can impact the way schools interact with and aid these families. Moreover, African American families have socio-economic obstacles, such as precarious housing or employment, which can impede their ability to participate in their children's education according to conventional school expectations. The combination of these factors results in African American children encountering substantial obstacles right from the start of their educational journey (Berry, 2023; Iruka, 2022; Rashid, 2009). This perpetuates cycles of inequality and restricts their prospects for future achievement. Unconscious biases among educators can lead to African American children being given less encouragement, fewer chances for advanced learning, and lower expectations. Teachers may inadvertently engage in differential interactions with Black children, providing them with reduced compliments, less intellectually demanding tasks, and diminished focus, all of which can harm their academic self-perception and drive.

Many early childhood education programs fail to incorporate culturally relevant pedagogy that reflects and respects the experiences and histories of African American children. Therefore, creating additional systemic issues with early childhood education. The lack of representation can affect a child's sense of belonging and identity in the classroom and contribute to disengagement from the learning process. Therefore, culturally relevant pedagogy is imperative for children in early childhood.

Culturally relevant pedagogy emphasizes the importance of recognizing and valuing the cultural backgrounds of African American children. It involves creating a curriculum that reflects the children's histories, values, and experiences. By incorporating the culture, traditions, and historical perspectives into the curriculum, educators can help children see themselves in what they are learning, fostering a sense of belonging and engagement in the classroom. This type of learning aims to make early childhood education relevant and accessible by connecting educational content to children's lived experiences. As an educator, I know that when students see their culture and identity reflected in the curriculum, they are motivated and successful academically. This approach highlights the strengths and potential of the students.

When using culturally relevant pedagogy in early childhood centers it encourages critical thinking about social justice, racism, and inequalities. Introducing these concepts early can develop a critical consciousness. That helps students understand and navigate the world around them. African American children can be empowered and equipped with the tools to recognize and challenge systemic injustices. Teachers who practice culturally relevant pedagogy work to build strong, trusting relationships with students and their families. As an educator, you seek to understand the community and culture of the students you service. This helps create a supportive and responsive learning environment. For African American children, it is important for teachers to understand the culture and advocate for their needs within the educational system (Berry, 2023; Iruka, 2022; Rashid, 2009).

Culturally relevant pedagogy and educational justice are interconnected because the goal creates an equitable and inclusive education system. Educators can begin addressing African American children's cultural and educational needs by implementing culturally relevant pedagogy. This lays the groundwork for broader educational justice. This approach ensures that African American children receive an education that not only respects their cultural identity but also actively works to dismantle the systemic barriers that have historically limited their educational opportunities. Early childhood education programs that are inclusive and culturally responsive contribute to social equity by ensuring that African American children are not marginalized within the education system. These programs promote a more equitable distribution of educational resources and opportunities, a fundamental goal of educational justice. Together, culturally relevant pedagogy and educational justice create a framework for early childhood education that is responsive to the needs of African American children and committed to fostering a more just and equitable society.

Early education that is culturally responsive, adequately funded, and free from bias can help mitigate these systemic inequities. When African American students receive equitable resources and support from the start, it can disrupt the cycle of inequitable educational practices that many face (Barnett et al., 2013; Berry, 2023; Iruka, 2022; Rashid, 2009).

Long-Term Educational Outcomes

African American children participating in engaging, culturally relevant, and unbiased early childhood education programs have significant long-term outcomes. This contributes to the broader goals of educational justice for this group of children who continue to deal with educational injustices.

Early childhood education provides African American children with foundational skills in literacy, numeracy, and critical thinking. These skills are crucial for success in the later grades. Children who attend high-quality early childhood programs are more likely to perform better academically throughout their school years. For African American children, who often face systemic challenges in education, these early gains can help close achievement gaps that tend to widen over time. By providing African American children with a strong start, early childhood education helps close the achievement gap between African American students and their peers. This is a key aspect of educational justice, which seeks to ensure that all children, regardless of their background, have an equal opportunity to succeed in school and life.

When children are immersed in an effective early childhood education program, it has lasting effects on language development. Early language skills are foundational to literacy, comprehension, and overall academic success. Furthermore, children with strong language abilities are better equipped to engage with the curriculum. This prepares children for the academic demands of formal schooling. Therefore, children from underserved communities who enter school with strong language skills are less likely to face barriers that often lead to academic underachievement. When focused on language development in early childhood, it helps close the achievement gap that often exists between children from different socioeconomic backgrounds. This is important for African American children who face systemic inequalities in educational outcomes.

Furthermore, African American children participating in early childhood programs will likely graduate from high school, attend college, and have higher lifetime earnings. Access to such programs is a form of educational justice, as it increases their opportunities for upward mobility and reduces the racial disparities in educational attainment and economic outcomes. This contributes to breaking the cycle of poverty and inequality.

Many African American children exposed to early childhood education help support their social and emotional development and long-term success in their well-being. They are better equipped to navigate the social dynamics of school and life. They can self-regulate and develop problem-solving abilities and interpersonal skills, which are essential for both academic and personal success. Children in effective early childhood programs are predicted to also engage in healthier behaviors. They have reduced stress and anxiety because the children are in a stable, supportive environment that helps them develop to their fullest potential. Early childhood education programs that are inclusive and culturally responsive contribute to social equity by ensuring that African American children are not marginalized within the education system (Barnett et al., 2013; Berry, 2023; Iruka, 2022; Rashid, 2009). These programs promote a more equitable distribution of educational resources and opportunities, which is a fundamental goal of educational justice.

One of early childhood education's most profound long-term outcomes is its potential to reduce involvement with the criminal justice system. African American children who attend high-quality early education programs are less likely to engage in criminal behavior as adolescents and adults. This reduction in criminal justice involvement is linked to the early development of social skills, academic success, and positive relationships with peers and adults. By addressing root causes of criminal behavior—such as educational inequity and social exclusion—early childhood education contributes to a more just society where African American children are less likely to be funneled into the school-to-prison pipeline.

Educational justice is also about empowering African American communities by ensuring that their children have access to the resources and opportunities they need to succeed. When African American children thrive in early education, it strengthens the community as a whole, leading to greater collective advocacy for equitable policies and practices in education. Children who succeed academically and socially are more likely to become engaged and active citizens. For African American children, early educational success can lead to greater civic participation and leadership in their communities. This is vital for educational justice, as it ensures that African American voices and perspectives are represented in the broader societal discourse, including in the formulation of education policy.

The long-term outcomes of early childhood education for African American children are profound, spanning academic achievement, social-emotional development, health, and reduced criminal justice involvement. These outcomes contribute significantly to the advancement of educational justice by promoting equity, breaking cycles of poverty, and empowering African American communities. By investing in early childhood education, society can move closer to a more just and equitable education system where all children, regardless of race, have the opportunity to reach their full potential.

Community and Societal Impact

Societal inequities, including systemic racism, often manifest in the education system through discriminatory practices, biased curriculum, and unequal access to quality education. These factors contribute to the achievement gap between African American students and their peers. Addressing the impact of community and societal factors is essential for achieving educational justice for African American students. It requires a concerted effort from educators, policymakers, communities, and society to dismantle the barriers that impede academic success and create an equitable educational landscape. Therefore, community and societal environments significantly shape African American students' educational experiences and outcomes. Understanding these impacts is crucial.

When schools partner with local organizations, they can provide resources and services to African American families. They can support academic success and the overall well-being of students and their families. This includes after-school programs, health services, mentorship, and family engagement initiatives. Mentorship within the community can offer African American students role models who understand their cultural background and challenges. This can help boost academic motivation and self-esteem. When parents and community members actively participate in school activities, it ensures that the school's policies and practices are responsive to the needs of African American students.

Societal inequities, including systemic racism, often manifest in the education system through discriminatory practices, biased curriculum, and unequal access to quality education (Thomas-Jones, 2024). These factors contribute to the achievement gap between African Americans and their peers. Therefore, many African American communities face economic challenges that affect educational opportunities. Schools in economically disadvantaged areas often lack adequate funding, leading to fewer resources, larger class sizes, and outdated materials. Furthermore, housing segregation continues to impact African American students by confining many under-resourced schools in segregated neighborhoods. This limits their access to high-quality education and perpetuates cycles of poverty.

When African American children are exposed to a curriculum that reflects their history, culture, and contribution, it can enhance their sense of identity and belonging. This leads to higher engagement and academic achievement, which will have a positive impact on the community. A diverse teaching staff can positively impact African American students by providing role models and educators who relate to their experiences and cultural backgrounds. This type of diversity helps reduce biases in the classroom and begins closing the academic gap. Schools must prioritize cultural competence to improve community and societal impact further. Teachers and staff that are properly trained understand and respect their students' cultural backgrounds. This can help in creating an inclusive environment that supports all students.

Portraying African American students and communities in the media can influence public perceptions and policy decisions. Positive representation can help combat stereotypes and build support for educational equity. There are campaigns to raise awareness about the challenges faced by African American students and the importance of educational justice that can mobilize community support and influence policy. Therefore, addressing the impact of community and societal factors is essential for achieving educational justice for African American students. It requires a concerted effort from educators, policymakers, communities, and society to dismantle the barriers that impede academic success and create an equitable educational landscape.

Bumps on the Road to Educational Justice

Several years ago, I went on a road trip with my family. The trip was planned to take 16 hours, allowing for stops for food and gas. We knew there could be some minor delays, but we didn't expect the number of issues that arose along the way. First, the bus got a flat tire. Then, the bathroom needed repairs. Finally, a problem with the transmission prevented us from going over 55 miles per hour. What should have been a 16-hour journey stretched into 22 hours, causing frustrations for everyone. I use this story as a parallel to the journey toward educational justice. Many assume that achieving educational justice is straightforward, but like my family trip, unforeseen roadblocks can slow or derail progress. Challenges such as inequitable policies, funding limitations, underqualified teachers, and systemic biases act as flat tires and transmission issues on the road to just and accessible education. Recognizing and addressing these obstacles is crucial to overcoming them and reaching our destination of true educational equity.

Just as my family's road trip encountered unexpected delays that prolonged our journey, many African American children face early roadblocks that extend the time and effort required to reach their goals. Without early academic support from educators, administrators, and stakeholders, these children face setbacks that limit their educational and economic opportunities. These are like a flat tire or transmission issue that slows down a journey. These challenges don't just delay individual progress. They contribute to an intergenerational cycle of poverty and inequality. When children fall behind in their education, they're more likely to face academic hardships as adults, which affects their ability to support the next generation's educational needs. In this way, each setback compounds over time, perpetuating a cycle of disadvantage that is difficult to overcome. Recognizing these barriers is essential to helping all students reach their educational justice and equity destination.

My family found themselves on a never-ending trip, and at each turn, it offered additional obstacles, and so did the educational journey for African American children in early education. These significant roadblocks continue to have barriers like poverty, exposure to trauma, and limited access to quality resources. These obstacles delay their progress and threaten to create lasting setbacks. Therefore, quality early education can help clear the road ahead, offering a stable, enriched environment that supports healthy development and empowers students to overcome these initial disadvantages.

The road to educational justice is a winding road with lots of stops, detours, and roadblocks. Therefore, investing in equitable early education benefits not just individual students but also entire communities, leading to increased economic stability, reduced crime, and greater civic engagement. Prioritizing the early education of African American children is an essential step toward creating a just and equitable education system. As a society, we have a choice. Allow these roadblocks to continue to hinder progress or use education as a powerful tool to pave the way for lasting educational justice and equity.

Figure 1.
Road to Educational Justice

Note: The author created this figure.

The Time is Now for Educational Justice

Early childhood education is the foundation of every child's long-term academic and personal development. This is significantly profound for African American children in urban schools. During these formative years, children develop the building blocks for cognitive, social, and emotional growth. It shapes their future learning and life experience. For too long, systemic barriers and inequities have denied African American children access to high-quality education. The denial of access perpetuates a cycle that affects their academic achievement and impacts their life outcomes.

There are evident disparities that impact early childhood education. African American children have less experienced teachers and lack enriching curriculum and culturally responsive practices. These inequities are not mere accidents. They are products of policies and practices that uphold racial and socioeconomic divides. As a result, African American children enter kindergarten without the same opportunities for early learning and development as their peers. This puts them at an immediate disadvantage and widens the achievement gap early.

The time for educational justice is now. Addressing the inequities in early childhood is not just policy reform. There is a need for immediate action while reframing the conversation around early childhood education. We need to prioritize justice to ensure that African American children have access to effective and supportive early childhood development, affirming their identity while setting them on a path toward academic and personal success. Achieving justice goes beyond equal access to early childhood education. It requires school districts and stakeholders to invest in programs that specifically meet the needs of African American children.

Committing to educational justice in the early years is imperative. It is the first step to dismantling educational injustices. It allows children, regardless of their background, to realize their full potential. Therefore, the moment of change is now. Educators and other stakeholders must act now to ensure that African American children receive the early childhood education they deserve. When there is a commitment to educational justice, it fulfills the promise to build a just and equitable education for generations to come.

CHAPTER 3: LITERACY

Some years ago, I met an educator with a deep passion for teaching reading. Her daily mantra was teaching reading to children. This reflected her commitment and awareness that for her students to have opportunities, they needed to read proficiently by the end of first grade. Yet she often expressed concern for her students. She realized that too many African American children, especially those deeply affected by the pandemic, lacked the support necessary to close the literacy gap and catch up to grade level. For African American children in urban areas, literacy represents not only an academic skill but a foundation for educational equity.

Many educators share her sense of urgency, working tirelessly to implement strategies to improve literacy. These educators go beyond school hours to tutor students and engage families. However, literacy remains a significant challenge within the African American community. Conversations with families often reveal a complicated relationship with reading. For many, it feels like a force in school but a reluctant choice at home. Societal pressures add to this challenge. We often say, "Readers are Leaders," and many African American children struggle to connect with this idea. Many overwhelming societal issues make literacy feel less urgent in many homes.

To address these barriers, we must start from the ground up. Addressing both the literacy and societal challenges that affect African American communities. It will take a collective commitment from educators, families, community leaders, and policymakers to promote and model the importance of reading. Only through this concerted effort by implementing evidence-based literacy strategies in the classroom, working closely with families to build a culture of reading, and providing families with resources and support to foster literacy at home supports closing the academic gap and move toward true educational justice for African American children. Educational justice through literacy is about more than helping individual students. It's about transforming communities. When African American children have equitable access to literacy, they're empowered with the skills they need to thrive, pursue opportunities, and become leaders who give back to their community.

African American Experience with Literacy

During the period of slavery in the United States, enslaved African Americans were systematically denied access to education, including learning to read and write. This had a profound and devastating impact on literacy among all, particularly children. Many Southern states enacted laws that did not permit the education of enslaved people. In 1831, after Nat Turner's Rebellion, the state of Virginia passed a law making it illegal to teach enslaved individuals to read and write. Similar laws existed in other states. There were severe penalties for those who violated the law. This was intended to maintain control over the enslaved population. This was an attempt to prevent African Americans from gaining knowledge that could lead to rebellion or escape.

Racial ideology during slavery was used to justify the denial of education. The thoughts of the masses were that African Americans were inherently inferior and incapable of learning. These thoughts further entrenched the systemic oppression of African Americans. Therefore, even where there were explicit legal barriers, enslaved children had no access to educational resources. They were required to work from a very young age, leaving little time for learning.

Additionally, there were no schools for enslaved children, and their parents, even if literate, had limited time and resources to teach them. Despite these barriers, some enslaved people pursued an education in secret. They meet in unusual places, like the woods or an enslaved person's home. A person from the community who was literate would teach the others in the community. Literacy was seen as a tool for empowerment and a pathway to freedom. Therefore, it was seen as an act of resistance.

The impact of slavery on literacy extended well beyond the abolishment of slavery. After the Civil War, African Americans in the South faced enormous challenges in accessing education due to segregation. Many schools for African Americans were underfunded and faced ongoing challenges of discrimination. The gap in literacy that originated during slavery has had a generational impact. This long-lasting effect continues to shape the educational landscape for African American children for decades, if not centuries, to come.

In the present day and age, history continues to repeat itself when it comes to African American children and literacy. The past and present struggles are the children are subjected to segregated and underfunded schools, which have had long-lasting effects on their literacy development. The lack of basic resources, including books, qualified teachers, and educational materials, is critical for fostering literacy skills. However, literacy is not just a systemic issue or educational concern. It is a matter of social justice (Ashford-Hanserd et al., 2020; Perkins & Cooter, 2005). Therefore, in many schools, the curriculum has traditionally been Eurocentric. This often-marginalized African American literature and history. The lack of representation can lower engagement and achievement for African American children.

African American children are disproportionately affected by poverty, which limits access to books and early literacy experiences at home. Therefore, these children often have less access to effective literacy programs, contributing to the literacy gap that begins before kindergarten. So, early exposure is critical to reading and strongly predicts later academic success. The lack of literacy exposure at an early age adds to African American students not receiving equitable instruction (Straus, 2011). When these children have access to high-quality early childhood education, it helps develop foundational literacy skills.

In speaking with educators, it was concluded that literacy challenges contribute to significant achievement gaps between African American children and their peers. These gaps are reflected in standardized test scores, graduation rates, and college enrollment. African American children's low literacy levels are connected to dropout rates and increased involvement with the criminal justice system. A child's literacy level impact the school-to-prison pipeline. Limited exposure to literacy continues the cycles of poverty and disenfranchisement. Literacy affects all areas of learning. Therefore, African American children with low literacy skills are less likely to perform well in other subjects, limiting their opportunities for higher education and well-paying jobs (Ladson-Billings, 2009).

This requires families, schools, and stakeholders to do things differently to improve this major issue in education. Therefore, African American culture and history should be incorporated into the curriculum. This can enhance African American students' engagement and literacy outcomes.

Culturally relevant pedagogy recognizes the importance of students' culture in all aspects of learning. Literacy extends beyond the basic ability to read and write. It encompasses critical thinking, the capacity to engage with culturally relevant materials, and the ability to communicate effectively (Barnes, 2021). When you engage families and communities with literacy development programs, literacy has significantly improved. Programs that include access to books, literacy workshops, and support networks have proven to be effective tools for families. It is imperative that society address the systemic inequities that can contribute to the literacy gap. This requires developing comprehensive intervention policies, equitable funding for schools, early education programs, and support for teachers in delivering culturally responsive instruction.

Improving literacy outcomes for African American children is essential for achieving educational justice. Literacy is not just about reading and writing; it is about empowering students to access and participate fully in society. Without addressing the literacy challenges that African American students face, the broader goals of educational justice cannot be realized.

Literacy as a Gateway to Academic Success

While engaged in the writing process of this book, I found myself seated on the beach and saw two key occurrences. An initial observation was that children and families were laughing and enjoying the day. The second observation was that individuals seated in the beach chairs were completely engrossed in reading a novel. It encompassed not just the adults but also the children. I did not overhear parents engaging in negotiations with children over reading. A mother was engaged in the act of reading a novel to her son.

My heart was brimming with absolute delight as it confirmed that individuals have a strong affinity for reading. Allow me to clarify that the individuals present on the beach engaged in reading were exclusively White parents and children. A significant number of African American children lack exposure to leisure reading materials that foster the development of a passion for reading. Most of the time, they only have exposure to reading in school.

Socioeconomic, cultural, and historical factors influence the differences in reading engagement between White and African American families. I need to note that White families have higher income levels and more access to educational resources like books, libraries, and high-quality schools, which contributes to their greater engagement in reading. However, many African American families are more likely to experience economic hardships, which leads to longer working hours for parents. This leads to less time for direct involvement in reading activities with their children. Many white people frequently use reading materials that align with mainstream educational systems. African American families emphasize oral traditions, storytelling, and culturally relevant texts that reflect their experiences. Historically, reading materials have lacked African American representation, which can impact engagement. If children don't see themselves in the stories they read. They might feel less connected to the material.

Schools serving predominantly African American communities tend to have fewer resources, which means less encouragement of reading both at school and at home. White children, on the other hand, benefit from better-funded schools with robust literacy programs. Therefore, many teachers have lower expectations for African American children. This influences the type of reading assignments given and the support provided to families for at-home reading. The differences between families and cultural dynamics impact how children engage with reading. Reading is considered the gateway to everything we need. As the older people would say, "Reading is fundamental." Therefore, we need to instill this fundamental skill in African American children because it will allow them to navigate the world we live in. White children receive these fundamental skills at a very early age. They do not consider reading a chore but an adventure.

The U.S. Department of Education, through the National Assessment of Educational Progress (NAEP), has reported that African American children in urban schools typically score lower on reading assessments than their White and Asian peers. NAEP noted that only 18% of African American 4th graders and 15% of 8th graders scored at or above the proficient level in reading. This compared to 45% of White students and around 60% of Asian students who scored proficient or above. The gap tends to be most pronounced at the 4th and 8th grade levels, which are key assessment points. These disparities underscore the ongoing need for targeted interventions to support African American children, and close the achievement gaps

Literacy is tied to children's success because it forms the foundation for all learning. For African American children, literacy is particularly crucial because it equips them with the tools needed to navigate and challenge the systemic barriers they may face throughout their education and beyond. Therefore, many children have not been exposed to effective literacy strategies, so they are not literate. When a person is literate, that encompasses more than the ability to read. It's the capacity to critically comprehend, analyze, and engage with the text. This is essential for academic achievement and self-advocacy.

Many African American children are not literate by the first grade, which is a predictor of later academic achievement. A child falling behind at this stage can lead to a cumulative disadvantage. This can significantly impact the self-esteem and confidence of African American children, which can motivate them to take on new challenges. It also limits their ability to navigate the world around them and limits their voice in their communities and society at large. Therefore, ensuring African American children are literate by first grade is an educational priority. It equips them with the skills and confidence needed to navigate and succeed in a world that often presents barriers to their progress.

Literacy is the cornerstone of academic success. It allows students to access and engage with the curriculum across all subjects. Without strong literacy skills, African American children are more likely to fall behind in school. This can lead to a cycle of underachievement, disengagement, and discouragement. Therefore, literate children are better equipped to advocate for themselves and their communities. They understand and question the world around them. They make informed decisions and express their needs and rights. This is particularly significant for African American children in a society where they face racial biases and inequalities. Literacy empowers this marginalized group of students to assert their identity, challenge microaggressions or stereotypes, and fight for equity.

Educational equity ensures that all students, regardless of their background, have access to the resources, opportunities, and support they need to succeed. Strong literacy skills can open doors and break cycles for African

American children. Therefore, disparities in literacy contribute to the achievement gap between African American children and their peers. When prioritizing literacy early, educators can close the achievement gap and ensure that African American children start their journey to educational justice on an equal footing.

Children who receive a strong foundation in literacy and engage with the rigorous and advanced curriculum are literate. However, some African American children are placed in remedial literacy classes because they do not consistently engage with literacy. These classes limit their educational exposure and reinforce systemic inequities. Ensuring that African American children achieve literacy allows them to participate fully in all aspects of education. Therefore, literate individuals are better equipped to challenge injustices, advocate for change, and contribute to society.

Connection Between Literacy and Discipline

At the beginning of my teaching career, I had a student who had many restrooms breaks whenever we began our reading lesson. He occupied the bathroom for 20 minutes. Upon return to class, he would select a classmate with whom to engage in physical altercations. After some weeks, I concluded that he had devised a defense mechanism to evade the topic he regarded as challenging. He intentionally left reading classes for several years to evade gaining reading skills. This was a symptom of the problem; other educators complained about his behavior and never discussed a solution. After discussing with the student, he told me that he found reading challenging and lacked interest. He also expressed his intention to never engage in it due to his aspirations to join the NFL.

This student's resistance to reading led to disciplinary problems. The connection between literacy and discipline in African American children is significant and multifaceted. Poor literacy skills often correlate with behavioral challenges in school, which can lead to disproportionate disciplinary measures for many African American children. Eventually, this student's behavior became overwhelming for the teachers and staff. He was transferred to an out-of-district school.

The facts are that this student was frustrated because of his low literacy skills when trying to keep up with his peers. Therefore, his frustration manifested as disruptive behavior and task avoidance in the classroom. This is true for other African American children. They feel embarrassed or inadequate and might act out to deflect attention from their academic difficulties. This type of response is typical for many African American children in urban areas. They disconnect from reading and have discipline issues during that class. Poor literacy skills correlate with behavioral challenges in school. This led to disproportionate disciplinary measures for many African American children.

Within the school system, African American children are often disciplined more harshly and frequently than their white peers. These students are perceived to have more disruptive and problematic behaviors that stem from academic struggles, such as reading difficulties. This connection between literacy struggles and discipline becomes a great problem. Instead of the students receiving academic support, they are suspended or expelled, further setting them back academically. Literacy and discipline require systemic changes. Schools must invest in literacy programs targeting children from marginalized communities. They should also adopt restorative justice practices to address behavioral issues more constructively (Banks, 2005; Bingham & Dean, 2023; Mesa et al., 2021).

The link between literacy, discipline, and long-term outcomes for African American students is also connected to the school-to-prison pipeline. Students who are suspended or expelled are more likely to fall behind. They either drop out of school or become entangled in the juvenile justice system. Low literacy and literacy rates among African American children, compounded by harsh disciplinary practices, contribute to this pipeline. This makes it harder for these students to escape cycles of poverty and marginalization in education and society. Improving literacy for African American children is an academic issue and a critical step in reducing disciplinary disparities and promoting long-term success. The next section discusses further the school-to-prison pipeline (Banks, 2005; Bingham & Dean, 2023; Mesa et al., 2021).

Reducing the School-to-Prison Pipeline

Prior to embarking on a career in education, I worked as a counselor at a correctional institution. I collaborated with incarcerated individuals who had been involved in the criminal justice system from their early years. Many individuals transitioned from minor infractions to serious crimes. During conversations with them, they would express their dissatisfaction with school, and a significant number of them hadn't finished high school. Examining it from an alternative perspective suggests a manifestation of a lack of connection between the educational institution and the students. Many African American males and females were without literacy skills and sought information regarding the educational curriculum provided by the judicial institution. Moreover, the investigation determined that many individuals did not gain the essential reading abilities in educational institutions.

The individuals I interviewed failed to establish a sense of connection with their teachers, resulting in a lack of commitment towards developing the necessary skills for academic success.

Therefore, there is a strong connection between literacy and the criminal justice system. Many educators and other stakeholders constantly discuss the connection because this is a major issue impacting student literacy development. This drives many educators to help improve African American literacy in the primary grades because of the school-to-prison pipeline connection. The school-to-prison pipeline pertains to policies and practices that tend to disproportionately push African American children to transition from the educational setting to the criminal justice system. African American children are repeatedly disadvantaged by their lagging performance in literacy courses. It has been noted that many of the children read up to three grade levels below. Therefore, promoting literacy is essential to tackling systematic disparities in the education and criminal justice systems (Chapman & Hobbel 2006; Delale, 2017; Grace & Nelsen, 2019; Jacobs et al., 2022).

The United States allocates a greater amount of funds to imprisoning individuals than to providing education to the youth, especially in economically disadvantaged communities (Martin & Beese, 2017). This disproportion of funding has significant implications for educational justice, especially for African American children. Schools in urban communities often lack basic resources when funds are diverted to incarceration. Underfunded schools perpetuate the continued cycle of poverty and limit African American children's opportunities to succeed academically.

The disadvantage of funding between schools and prisons prevents the hiring and retaining of qualified teachers, leading to teacher retention issues. This results in larger classroom sizes and less individualized attention given to students. This lowers the quality of education, which disproportionately affects African American children. Therefore, the funding imbalance contributes to the school-to-prison pipeline. Many African American children are impacted the most by the money being funneled out of the public schools into the criminal justice system. This reinforces the inequities towards this marginalized group of children. Urban schools are most likely to be underfunded, and the children who attend face barriers to academic success and higher chances of incarceration. This cycle of inequity undermines educational justice. African American children deserve equitable opportunities and resources to eliminate the barriers that prevent educational justice.

This funding disparity leads to long-term societal costs and undermines educational justice by perpetuating cycles of poverty and incarceration, particularly among African American children. Therefore, there must be a shift in priorities to achieve true educational justice. The greater emphasis is on investing in the education and development of children in marginalized communities. This will break the school-to-prison pipeline cycle and promote equity and opportunity for all.

When African American children struggle with reading and comprehension, they are likely to disengage from school. This leads to a high dropout rate and increases their vulnerability to the school-to-prison pipeline. Early literacy intervention is essential in preventing children from falling behind academically. Schools can help reduce these disparities

71

by supporting literacy development and creating a more inclusive and supportive educational environment. The literacy program should be engaging, reduce behavioral issues, and enhance their overall academic performance. When schools incorporate culturally relevant materials and teaching methods, literacy instruction can be engaging and relatable to African American children. This group of students must see themselves reflected in the curriculum, as it can increase their sense of belonging and motivation to succeed. This type of engagement is key to keeping African American students in school and out of the criminal system (Chapman & Hobbel 2006; Delale, 2017; Grace & Nelsen, 2019; Jacobs et al., 2022).

Literate children are self-advocates and able to resolve conflict. These skills help them navigate challenges in school and reduce the likelihood of disciplinary action. Schools can reduce the reliance on strict punitive practices by fostering a positive school environment where literacy is a tool for communication and understanding. Therefore, punitive practices are reduced when educators advocate for policies prioritizing literacy. This can lead to restorative justice that can create systemic changes. Schools that focus on rehabilitation and education rather than punishment can break the cycle that feeds the school-to-prison pipeline. Literacy is a powerful tool that empowers African American children, educators, and communities to disrupt the cycles that feed the school-to-prison pipeline. This creates more equitable opportunities for all students.

There is a strong correlation between literacy rates and involvement in the juvenile justice system. Students who struggle with literacy are more likely to become disengaged from school, leading to higher dropout rates and an increased risk of incarceration. Addressing literacy challenges is a key strategy in disrupting the school-to-prison pipeline.

The connection between the educators and the students is the way out of the oppressive system of the school-to-prison pipeline. This is a vicious cycle for many African American children. These children are perceived as criminals or prospective criminals; their academic underachievement is then attributed to them, their culture, or their family, not a system that inherently hinders them. Many times, society relieved itself from its responsibility to address the educational system that hindered African American children from obtaining a free and suitable education.

Preventing Marginalization

African American children residing in urban areas have faced substantial marginalization in terms of literacy. The majority of children read material two to three grade levels below their white peers. School districts strive to implement targeted initiatives. Nevertheless, their influence is not universal among all children. As educational stakeholders, it is imperative to develop strategies to reduce these children's marginalization in literacy. Literacy grants immediate access to all knowledge and information available worldwide.

In the pursuit of educational equity, it is essential for educators and other relevant stakeholders to actively avoid the exclusion of African American children in the field of literacy instruction. Adopting a comprehensive strategy to tackle the structural obstacles that impede student literacy development is necessary. To effectively tackle the gap that leads to unequal educational chances for African American students in literacy, it is essential to thoroughly analyze past injustices, socioeconomic causes, institutional biases, and cultural importance (Perkins & Cooter, 2005). There is a well-established correlation between literacy and academic achievement, which has enduring impacts on educational results (Ready & Chu, 2015). Insufficient early exposure to reading leads to the unequal distribution of schooling among African American children (Straus, 2011). The application of segregation and discriminatory policies has exacerbated disparities in the educational opportunities provided to African American children, therefore directly impacting their literacy development (Ashford-Hanserd et al., 2020). Furthermore, to prevent the limited progress of reading abilities among African American children, it is imperative to enforce targeted interventions in educational institutions and the community.

Schools must prioritize the development of African American children's fluency in reading by highlighting their areas of proficiency instead of fixating on shortcomings. When instructors emphasize the strengths of kids, it fosters a sense of self-efficacy. A strong literacy identity is crucial for African American children to reduce marginalization. A significant number of students experience challenges in self-efficacy when learning to read. It is necessary to encourage appropriate participation in literacy activities. Establishing mentorship and tutoring programs focusing on literacy can provide African American children with support outside the classroom. These programs are powerful, especially when mentors share backgrounds similar to the students. This helps eliminate self-efficacy issues many African American children experience. When a mentor is relatable, it helps improve their literacy. Literacy tutors can provide one-to-one support to struggling readers. This can help prevent them from falling behind.

The literacy curriculum in schools should reflect diverse experiences to prevent marginalization. The history and culture of African American children are important when trying to improve their literacy. Culturally relevant teaching fosters a connection between their background and the material used in the classrooms. This makes literacy instruction more engaging and meaningful. African American children's marginalization in literature leads to disengagement. Therefore, African American children need access to high-quality reading materials. There should be books that reflect their identities and those that introduce them to diverse perspectives.

Teachers who are able to meet the diverse needs of African American children are imperative. Recognizing literacy gaps early and using teaching strategies that promote equity. Teachers should support struggling African American children with literacy without stigmatizing them. Education institutions prioritizing African American children's reading proficiency frequently pinpoint deficiencies, gather and evaluate data, and execute remedies. Educators empowered by data adapt their literacy instruction to meet the individual requirements of the students. Urban schools should employ culturally relevant and unbiased screenings to provide a precise understanding of the literacy development of African American children. Educators must guarantee that interventions are equitable and effective. Therefore, educators have a critical role in preventing literacy.

A comprehensive approach that addresses individual and systemic challenges is necessary to prevent the marginalization of African American children in literacy. Promoting early literacy intervention is crucial. Therefore, culturally relevant education must fuel the students, learning environments. Eliminating discriminatory bias requires educators, stakeholders, and families to develop meaningful community relationships. Providing opportunities and resources to African American children can effectively facilitate their success within the educational system and society. This will allow the children to be liberated and empowered to be productive within the community. Achieving educational justice requires prioritizing literacy equity as a fundamental measure to eliminate the historical challenges that have disenfranchised African American children.

Closing the Achievement Gap

Beginning in the early 2000s, students in New Jersey ranging from 3rd to 11th grade were administered the New Jersey Assessment Skill and Knowledge test. A considerable number of African American children attending urban schools did not achieve proficient scores. Consequently, numerous urban schools in New Jersey were categorized as schools that required improvement. After educators collaborated to analyze the test data, it was ascertained that there existed a significant gap in the literature compared to children residing in non-urban areas. Numerous districts implemented measures to narrow the gap in academic performance. As time advanced, it became evident that the strategies did not produce the desired outcomes for the districts.

With the writing of this book, I critically examine the methods and instruments utilized to address the academic gap in literacy. Enhanced efficacy of the approaches would result in a higher proportion of African American children achieving reading proficiency at or above grade level in urban schools. I am not proposing that teachers bear exclusive responsibility for bridging the academic gap. This requires a team effort from both family members and other appropriate individuals.

Many urban school systems mandate the assignment of literacy coaches, teachers, and tutors to address and decrease the literacy gap. Many educators enthusiastically tackle this work, while others perceive it as unattainable due to their biases. Nevertheless, providing these children with means to narrow the gap in literacy performance is imperative. To achieve this, all parties involved must take a proactive stance and endeavor to identify methods that address the injustices responsible for these discrepancies. The long-standing system of unequal literacy practices has had a significant influence on African American children.

In order to pursue educational justice for African American children, closing the literacy achievement gap is a crucial step. Academic success is measured by literacy skills and the ability to engage meaningfully in society. When there is a gap in literacy skills, there are far-reaching consequences for African American children. This has long-term academic, economic, and social outcomes. By prioritizing literacy, educators and communities can help dismantle barriers to educational equity. It can help foster a more just and inclusive learning environment for African American children.

Inconsistent allotment of resources and advocacy at the local, state, and federal levels in schools that primarily focus on African American communities directly influence the level of literacy instruction provided. Schools with insufficient funding frequently lack resources, inadequate instructional materials, and restricted availability of highly qualified teachers, resulting in diminished reading achievements. To address the gap in literacy rates, governments should support balanced and impartial funding mechanisms that guarantee schools in disadvantaged neighborhoods have equal opportunities to access top-notch resources, technology, and professional growth as wealthier schools. Therefore, there is a need to advocate for accountability to close the literacy gaps and eliminate discriminatory educational practices.

Closing the literacy achievement gap for African American children is not just a matter of improving testing scores. It is about securing educational justice and allowing children to succeed. There is a strong need to address systemic inequities by promoting culturally relevant instruction, engaging families, and advocating for policies that create a path to literacy equity. This work is essential to ensure that African American children are empowered with skills, knowledge, and confidence to thrive in school and within the community. This will break the cycle of marginalization and give African American children the educational justice they deserve.

The Need for Educational Justice

When African American children are introduced to literature early, it shapes their academic trajectory. In urban schools, access to diverse, culturally relevant, and affirming literature is more than an educational tool. It is a gateway to self-understanding, empowerment, and resilience in the face of systemic educational challenges. When African American children are exposed to literature early, it validates their abilities and aspirations. They can envision themselves in a world where they are capable of greatness. However, the exposure to literature early removes the systemic barriers these children face. The exclusion of a robust literacy program contributes to a sense of alienation and inferiority, reinforcing stereotypes and limiting academic engagement. African

American children often lack opportunities to develop critical literacy skills and a strong sense of cultural pride.

The time for educational justice is now for African American children. The stakes have never been higher. Society continues to grapple with persistent racial and educational disparities. There is an urgent need to reimagine the role of early literature exposure in promoting equity and justice. Achieving educational justice means creating a learning environment where African American children can access literature that tells their stories and equips them with the critical tools to question, resist, and redefine oppressive narratives. Justice fosters spaces where the children's voices are heard and valued. Their intellectual and creative abilities are nurtured and celebrated. Early literature becomes a powerful catalyst for change when educational justice is achieved. It cultivates confident, informed, and engaged children prepared to shape a more just and equitable future. It is important that educators and stakeholders seize the moment to advocate for educational justice. The need to champion early literacy affirms the identities of African American children and paves the way for systemic transformation. Justice ensures that every child, regardless of their background, has access to a high-quality, inclusive, and effective education.

CHAPTER 4: BIAS

Are you familiar with Ice Cube's song "Check Yo Self"? In one song, he raps the lyric, "You better check yourself before you wreck yourself!" As an educator, this serves as my bias evaluation statement, as our microaggressions and biases may hinder our capacity to engage effectively with students from urban districts. A bias checker promotes self-awareness and introspection. Educators must critically evaluate and confront biases against African American children. Many teachers may be unaware of their inherent biases. These biases affect teacher conduct and decision-making in the classroom. A daily "Check Yo Self" urges educators to introspect on their views, biases, and assumptions to recognize any potential biases they may possess. Upon self-reflection, instructors can prevent undermining the educational experience of African American children. This prevents them from spreading biases that adversely affect students' academic achievement and self-esteem. Educators can cultivate stronger and more equitable relationships with African American children by assessing their behaviors and intentions. This will create an inclusive educational atmosphere where all students feel valued and appreciated.

We have biases, and it is imperative that we address them before, during, and after our day in the classroom. Our biases can either make or break our interaction with our students. We must build relationships that are void of biases.

To establish equity, it is necessary to remove biases and assumptions regarding African American children (Linton, 2011; Stembridge, 2020). (Warikoo et al. 2016) found that a significant number of teachers exhibit a moderate to substantial level of bias toward African American children. Bias emerges from fear rather than authentic experiences, according to Linton (2011). Most biases arise from multifaceted stereotypes people have constantly been exposed to throughout their lives, further explored by Linton (2011). Many teachers feel inadequate to impart knowledge to children from various cultural and socioeconomic backgrounds. In their studies, Linton (2011) and Lorenzetti & Johnson (2022) observed that certain White middle-class educators have constraints in advancing equity because of their limited connections and personal experiences with persons from other backgrounds. A considerable proportion of these teachers lack a thorough understanding of educational justice. Therefore, their implicit bias can negatively impact students' academic performance and pose challenges during teacher interactions (Warikoo et al., 2016).

Numerous school districts in the United States exhibit a notable discrepancy in the racial and ethnic makeup of teachers and African American children. Schaeffer (2021) reports that Caucasian teachers represent 69% of the teaching staff in urban schools. Moreover, Barnes (2021) noted that specific white educators hold a privilege associated with their whiteness and conform to cultural norms that marginalize African American children. African-American children's academic achievements and educational attainment vary from those of their White counterparts (O'Keefe et al., 2019). Linton (2011) and Lorenzetti & Johnson (2022) argue that individuals form preconceived notions and biases against those who are different from them due to our inherent tendency to perceive them in connection to ourselves. Furthermore, Stembridge (2020) argues that if our biases and natural assumptions are not acknowledged, they can weaken educators' academic interaction with culturally diverse children. Thus, Aguilar (2020) emphasizes the need to address the cognitive, emotional, and belief systems of all individuals employed in school systems to bring about positive transformations in the experiences and achievements of African American children.

Educators let their personal biases and prejudices impact their instructional practices, particularly when dealing with African American children, and it hinders their ability to provide educational justice (Ashford-Hanserd et al., 2020; Ellerbrook et al., 2016; Evans et al., 2020; Linton 2011; Stembridge, 2020). According to Lorenzetti and Johnson (2022) and Stembridge (2020), educators with prejudices tend to have lower expectations for children who deviate from the well-behaved, ideal students. A considerable number of teachers fail to address their own biases (Lorenzetti & Johnson, 2020). As a result, educators prioritize behavior over equitable instruction implementations (Chin, 2020; Gregory et al., 2020; Lorenzetti & Johnson, 2022). These teachers instruct African American children at a level below their appropriate grade. Educational professionals should acknowledge the presence of biases and try to eliminate any biases hindering their capacity to deliver equitable and unbiased education (Ashford-Hanserd et al., 2020; Linton, 2011).

Implicit

As an educator, I have overheard educators' conversations where they assume that African American children are academically incapable than their White peers, leading to less support or lower expectations. These educators harbor negative assumptions or stereotypes about African American children. It manifests in their interactions, expectations, and instructional choices. Therefore, implicit bias is an attitude or stereotype that unconsciously affects understanding, actions, and decisions. These biases occur automatically and without conscious awareness. Implicit bias significantly impacts African American children within the educational system. It influences the decisions, actions, and expectations of educators and other stakeholders in the educational system, often in ways that perpetuate inequities and prevent academic progress. Teachers' implicit biases often result in lower academic expectations for African American children. Educators may unconsciously assume this group of children is less capable of high academic achievement and are not challenged academically. Educators and other stakeholders often stifle their potential. Educational justice requires that all students be held to high standards and given the resources and support to meet the needs of African American children. However, as long as implicit bias remains unchecked, African American children will continue to face structural disadvantages.

Implicit bias leads to systemic disparities in academic achievement for a particular group of children. African American children are less likely to receive the same quality of education as upper-class White children. This is solely attributed to biased expectations, unequal resource access, and discriminatory practices. These disparities persist throughout their academic journey. It limits their access to higher education and career opportunities. Therefore, closing the achievement gap ensures that African American children have the same opportunities for success as others is central to educational justice. Eliminating implicit bias at all levels of the educational system, from early childhood through higher education, is imperative.

Educators' implicit biases impact their interactions with African American families. This demographic of parents is perceived as having lower engagement or interest in their children's schooling. This results in inadequate communication and cooperation between the home and school environments. This contributes to the gap in learning due to educators' biased views towards African American children and their families. In order to create an inclusive environment where parents feel welcomed and appreciated as participants in their child's education, it is crucial to identify and confront implicit biases.

Every educational institution in the United States hosts Back to School night. The schools plan to engage with parents and people in the community. Nevertheless, in urban school districts, educators often hold preconceived ideas that parents will not participate. This is the underlying bias that affects familial interactions among African Americans. Insufficient parental presence or lack of concern for their child's education. In suburban locations, parents are provided with accommodations, and there are no preconceived ideas regarding nurturing and investing intellectually in their children. The inference is made that their parents had to work or were required to rearrange their schedules. Educators tend to exhibit more sympathy towards a White parent compared to an African American parent. This occurrence arises from the underlying biases we possess towards specific nationalities. Therefore, teachers and other stakeholders can achieve educational justice by cultivating more robust and reliable relationships free from implicit biases.

Implicit bias connects with the social-emotional development of African American children. These biases shape how educators, peers, and society interact with these children. There are negative assumptions about African American children's behavior, intelligence, or potential. When children are exposed to biased treatment or diminished expectations from educators and other stakeholders, they internalize a sense of inadequacy or inferiority. The consequences include diminished self-esteem and withdrawal from educational activities, which can lead to mistrust of the educational system. In the long run, have adverse effects on mental well-being.

When children are viewed through a biased lens of suspicion or deficit, it undermines their sense of belonging and safety within the educational system. The nature of bias creates emotional barriers to learning and social-emotional interaction. African American children are subjected to lower expectations and harsh discipline. The educational system fails to nurture their potential. Implicit bias widens the educational gap, not because of students' abilities but because the educational system works against them.

African American children who attend academic settings free from implicit bias foster learning and experience a sense of worth and prestige. Resolving implicit bias is crucial for establishing schools that promote the social-emotional welfare of African American children. Modifying an educator's outlook on implicit bias can promote equitable educational opportunities for African American children.

Throughout my extensive 20-year career in education, I have observed educators exhibiting implicit bias toward African American children that diminished their cultural relevance. Consequently, many teachers have no connection to the culture of the children they service, affecting the allocation of school resources and the curriculum that is implemented. Such circumstances result in misinterpretation of students' actions, language, family arrangements, unjust treatment, or an inability to establish meaningful connections with students. The curriculum consistently eliminates or marginalizes African American history, literature, and contributions. However, their access to competent teachers and advanced courses is limited because of the influence of implicit bias on school finance and curriculum. African American children have greater difficulty in seeing their own identities mirrored in their everyday educational endeavors. By suppressing the student's identity while the educator is unintentionally oblivious to their actions and failing to address the underlying assumptions that result in inadequate resources for African American children. This kind of implicit bias compounds educational inequity. Therefore, when African American children see their culture and history accurately portrayed in their education, together with sufficient financial resources for schools, they are more inclined to participate and experience a sense of worth.

Implicit bias undermines the educational experiences and outcomes of African American children. It reinforces harmful stereotypes. It creates barriers that prevent academic success and perpetuate the continued inequities in treatment and opportunities. Therefore, to achieve educational justice, stakeholders must address these biases. That requires training, policy changes, and an academic environment where all students can thrive. Schools can take meaningful steps toward closing the achievement gap by recognizing and confronting implicit bias. This will ensure that African American children receive the equitable education they deserve. Furthermore, true educational justice cannot be achieved until we create an environment where African American children are seen, valued, and supported as they deserve.

Explicit Bias

It is assumed that educators in urban schools are unbiased while engaging with African American students. Nonetheless, that is not always the situation. Numerous educators possess biases toward the students they instruct. They evaluate them severely, make derogatory remarks, and are extremely punishing in their disciplinary actions towards the children. Some may articulate that they instruct in urban districts due to a more favorable wage scale compared to numerous suburban districts. The intentional biases of these educators foster academic inequalities against African American children.

At the onset of my teaching career, I met an educator who had instructed at many different schools. She began teaching at a new school system or charter school every two to three years. In discussions on her experience, she consistently expressed negative feelings about the children she instructed. One day, students arrived to class furious because of the teacher's racist comments toward the African American children she was instructing. Her comments were highly disrespectful, and the children were angry because she failed to see them as motivated learners. She perceived them as criminals, dropouts, substance abusers, and other stereotypical clichés. The children had exhausted their patience that day, and one student made quite insulting remarks to her. The child was referred to the office and received a five-day suspension. The students were disrespectful, and it was concluded that the teacher's explicit biases provoked the child's response. The sole decision available to this student was that the teacher would not return for the subsequent academic year. Nonetheless, the mental harm had already been inflicted upon these African American students in this urban school.

Explicit bias encompasses conscious and overt prejudice or discriminating beliefs. This can adversely affect educational equity for African American students. Explicit bias is evident in intentional acts, policies, or attitudes that adversely impact the educational experience of African American children. Explicit bias compromises educational equity since underprivileged children experience inequitable treatment in the classroom. African American children are subjected to racist policies and behaviors. Consequently, children are acquiring knowledge in an adversarial educational setting due to overt prejudices. This results in obstacles being established to hinder advanced learning chances. Moreover, it diminishes the quality of education provided to African American children due to misconceptions.

Educators with clear prejudices differentiate their treatment of African American children compared to their counterparts. This is evident in multiple forms, including diminished attention for students and more severe disciplinary measures. These children are afforded limited options for academic participation. Educators with explicit biases may deliberately perceive African American children as less capable or less worthy of academic assistance. This results in deliberate neglect or discriminatory actions within the classroom. Such tactics result in discriminatory policies and actions.

Explicit bias results in the implementation of discriminatory educational practices that disproportionately impact African American children. Numerous educational institutions implement zero-tolerance policies that impose severe penalties for small offenses. In some schools, dress standards are enforced, and depending on the enforcer, numerous African American children experience intimidation from school staff who exhibit explicit bias against them. Recently, hair prohibitions have been implemented in a manner that disproportionately affects African American children. These regulations originate from explicitly prejudiced perspectives regarding African American children. A significant portion of society perceives themselves as susceptible to violence, misconduct, and nonconformity. This exacerbates racial disparities in disciplinary measures and educational opportunities (Colby, 1985; Rucker & Jubilee, 2007; Yang et al., 2018).

African American children have faced hostile educational settings due to overt racism displayed by educators and/or peers. Incidents of racial harassment, disparaging insults, or exclusion based on race do occur. There are more teachers now making insensitive racial slurs towards and against the children they service. This leads children to view schools as unpleasant and sometimes dangerous environments. Therefore, explicit racism from educators or administrators may incite racially motivated bullying, therefore exacerbating the marginalization of African American children. In 2024, overt bias continues in educational institutions following the Jim Crow era (Colby, 1985; Rucker & Jubilee, 2007; Yang et al., 2018). This reinforces the jeopardization of academic advancement for African American youngsters. Educators and stakeholders exhibit an intentional bias against underprivileged students, while the current political climate increases underlying stereotypes.

Explicit bias often results in the marginalization of African American children from significant educational opportunities. They are omitted from gifted and talented programs, honors courses, and Advanced Placement classes.

Educators and school administrators intentionally perceive that African American children are incapable of handling rigorous academic material. Consequently, limiting or prohibiting their access to these services. This affects students' ability to succeed and supports biases in their educational achievement.

Furthermore, several lawmakers and school administrators with explicit biases regard the communities they serve as less deserving of educational funding, resulting in substandard educational facilities. Extracurricular opportunities are restricted, educational resources are outdated, and students' desks and chairs are in disrepair. When educators endorse or condone these discriminatory practices, it perpetuates detrimental stereotypes and marginalizes African American children. This diminishes their sense of identity and belonging inside the school system. Educational institutions that explicitly engage in racial discrimination exacerbate the systemic educational inequities encountered by African American children. This promotes inequities in schooling and denies African American children essential resources for academic achievement (Colby, 1985; Rucker & Jubilee, 2007; Yang et al., 2018).

Many educators wish to convey that explicitly bias against African American students is a memory of the past. They assert that the implemented laws have mitigated biases in educational settings. Nonetheless, this is not the case for numerous urban schools or African American children. Following the 2024 presidential debate, the blatantly discriminatory remarks made by the Republican candidate endangered a group of minority children. The remark was charged with prejudices and racial implications.

Consequently, it pushes others to reiterate biased statements. A significant number of these individuals are employed by public educational institutions and engage with minority students. If they express these racial sentiments privately, it is just a matter of time until these prejudices manifest in their teaching or within the school environment. Progress towards equal education seems to be consistently undermined, with every five steps forward met with ten steps backward

Educators must commit to rooting out discriminatory practices to ensure that African American children are treated with fairness, respect, and dignity across all aspects of their educational experience. Addressing explicit bias also requires ongoing training, reflection, and accountability to ensure that all practices promote equity and inclusion. This commitment is foundational to achieving educational justice and creating a system that uplifts every student. Therefore, tackling explicit bias is essential for achieving educational justice.

Microaggression

As an urban educator, I have witnessed daily microaggressions aimed at African American children. They often manifest quietly through mispronouncing their name or remarking on their speech. Many fail to see that as a microaggression. Consequently, they disregard it and strive to proceed as if it never occurred. Refusing to pronounce a child's name correctly or to comment on their speech reflects hidden and explicit biases, often dismissed as mere errors or oversights. What may be deemed trivial can have a profound impact on African American children. These provide the foundational elements of diminished self-esteem and identity concerns. These microaggressions perpetuate stereotypes, devalue cultural expressions, and render individuals feeling undervalued or disrespected. This leads to African American children experiencing exclusion or alienation within the academic environment.

In some cases, the microaggression may be evident. Certain educators diminish the intellectual capabilities of African American students, resulting in reduced expectations that adversely affect their confidence and motivation to pursue high-quality education. Microaggressions impair educational equity by perpetuating inequality, reinforcing systemic biases, and fostering a school environment that is less accepting or supportive of African American pupils. Microaggressions in educational environments present African American youngsters with further challenges. Unchecked microaggressions perpetuate ongoing injustice. It is harmful to undermine a child's hopes and dreams through our microaggressions against them.

Microaggressions can have a profound and detrimental impact on African American children in urban schools. This influences their educational experiences and contributes to broader issues of educational injustice. The subtle, often unconscious acts of discrimination can shape African American children's educational journey. African American children face constant exposure to microaggressions, such as being overlooked in class or hearing derogatory comments about racial background, which creates chronic stress. This stress results in anxiety, depression, low grades, and a lowered sense of self-worth (Barnes, 2021).

Because of microaggressions, African American children feel like outsiders in predominantly white or multicultural educational settings. This sense of exclusion affects the children's ability to engage in school activities fully. They are unable to foster meaningful relationships with teachers and peers. When teachers or staff dismiss the cultural backgrounds of African American students, it alienates their identities. Microaggressions lead to misunderstandings in students' speech patterns and cultural references that devalue them. This undermines their sense of belonging in the school, which is crucial for academic success. This makes many African American children feel ostracized by the educational system that should embraced them.

During the late 1980s and early 1990s, I was transported from my urban location to a suburban Catholic high school. The student body consisted of 70% Caucasians and 30% individuals from various ethnic backgrounds. Among that group, 30% of other African American children comprised less than 5% of the total school population. During that period, I experienced a direct lesson on microaggressions from educators and students. The religion instructor intentionally mispronounced my name. I corrected him daily, yet he repeated the mistake the following day. This was a nuanced yet significant indication that microaggression existed in this institution. The engagement with educators and peers consistently appeared forced due to underlying implications that the African American students were unwelcome. They embraced and revered the African American students who participated in basketball yet declined to recognize Black History Month. Experiencing frustration when seeking methods to address the microaggressions prevalent across the school. The microaggressions encountered at this school caused stress for every African American student. At the conclusion of the day, when we returned to the bus for our urban location, each student's collective sigh of relief signified the day's finish and our preservation of dignity.

Therefore, teachers may consciously or unconsciously assume that African American children are not as capable as others because of microaggressions. This leads to fewer opportunities for advanced coursework, leadership roles, and or other academic challenges. Over time, African American children who are constantly subjected to microaggressions become disengaged in school. The children feel their efforts are not valued by a system set up against them. This results in decreased academic motivation and overall lower achievement.

The need to address microaggressions in urban classrooms arises from their significant influence. Training is necessary for educators to identify and confront their own biases. Teachers must establish an inclusive and supportive classroom atmosphere, actively rejecting microaggressions. Thus, educational institutions should adopt varied curriculum that effectively combat the detrimental messages conveyed by microaggressions. The establishment of support networks by school systems for African American children may successfully reduce the negative effects of microaggressions. Microaggressions impact the day-to-day emotional and psychological well-being of African American pupils. This phenomenon exacerbates the educational inequity in metropolitan schools. To tackle these issues, it is necessary to implement structural changes prioritizing equity, inclusion, and cultural competence in education.

Imposter Syndrome

During my childhood, I remember a community program recruiting young African Americans to join the police and fire departments in Newark. This finally allowed many to embark on an unattainable law enforcement profession. Others interpreted the opportunity as a lack of desire to

95

police their acquaintances or fight fires in their neighborhood. While family members would encourage, it failed to persuade them to seize the opportunity. This puts limits on their potential and reinforces systemic inequities. The young men and women who refused the opportunity never made it out of the neighborhood that was plagued with drugs, violence, and low expectations. Their profound sense of exclusion results from their self-doubt and the judgments of others. In retrospect, a significant number of African American men and women experience imposter syndrome while attempting not to pursue that employment. Imposter syndrome also impacts children. Imposter syndrome causes this demographic to set lower academic or career goals. Many feel isolated or question their capabilities. Many African Americans internalize societal stereotypes. Many feel less intelligent, leading to decreased confidence in their academic abilities and career goals when they excel.

Therefore, imposter syndrome impacts African American children in education, especially in the context of the road to educational justice. Imposter syndrome refers to the internalized feeling of not belonging or underserving one's achievements. This is despite evidence of their competence. For African American children, this can manifest more intensely due to systemic factors, such as racial bias, discrimination, and the historical underrepresentation of African American students in advanced academic spaces. Imposter syndrome undermines African American children's potential by compounding the educational barriers they already face. To truly achieve educational justice, systems must address students' internal struggles. The external factors that exacerbate those feelings of being unworthy or incapable. Many African American children constantly question their place in educational spaces. This leads to higher levels of anxiety and stress. This emotional toll can impact academic performance. It impedes their personal well-being and hinders long-term educational aspirations.

Several years ago, while walking the school hallways, I overheard an African American student say to another student that he should have stayed home. It was 8:45 a.m., and school had only been in session for 30 minutes. This child already felt defeated. You could see it in his posture and engaging with the other students. My heart broke for this student because immediately, he felt like he did not deserve an education or feel safe academically or emotionally.

Further investigation revealed that this student confronted security, the principal, and the teacher. Each person asked, "Why did you come to school?" The insecurity for school is already present because he has a learning disability. This subtle yet profound microaggression towards this student enhanced his insecurity about school and his learning ability. Imposter syndrome manifests in middle school and is referred to as low self-esteem.

Experiencing imposter syndrome, African American children may choose to withdraw from advanced placement programs or promotions. They often feel undeserving of striving for great accomplishment. In order to limit their potential and perpetuate structural inequalities, they settle for mediocrity. The apprehension of being perceived as insufficient can hinder African American children from seeking assistance or making use of available resources. They actively refrain from engaging in scholarly debates. Many African American children possess a strong desire to demonstrate their inclusion in such environments by exhibiting self-sufficiency.

Education institutions should give top priority to establishing conducive conditions that foster a sense of belonging among African American children. This entails addressing and eradicating biased policies and practices and diverting subtle acts of disrespect that promote feelings of inferiority. The absence of African American educators and mentors contributes to imposter syndrome. It strengthens the notion that academic achievement is not well-suited for them. The growth of African American presence in the field of education can offer affirmation and motivation. The idea of imposter syndrome can worsen the educational setting if the experiences of African American children fail to represent diversity or acknowledge exceptional performance. An inclusive educational setting and well-trained educators acknowledge and address unconscious bias. Such action will facilitate the deconstruction of the feeling of estrangement. This can enhance the sense of visibility and worth among African American children.

Teacher Efficacy Issues

When there are biases present in classrooms, there are also teacher efficacy issues. Teachers' efficacy is closely intertwined with biases that shape how educators interact with students of different racial backgrounds. In my 20 years in education, the common thread is teacher efficacy because it directly affects students' performance, engagement, and motivation. Teachers with high self-efficacy are more likely to implement effective instructional strategies, manage classrooms efficiently, and foster positive relationships with students. When teacher efficacy is high there are improved academic outcomes for African American children. However, when efficacy is low there are lower expectations. There is a reduction in academic opportunities, less challenging coursework, and a lack of encouragement to purse advanced learning.

Researchers Thompson (2022), Sandoval et al. (2011), and Thomas-Jones (2024) identified that self-efficacy pertains to people's subjective assessments of their own competence. Therefore, self-efficacy mediates beliefs, motivation, and behavior, which plays a crucial part in education. Assessing the educators' degrees of self-efficacy is imperative to comprehend the influence of equitable teaching methods on African American students in urban districts. The teachers' self-efficacy level determines the academic success level for African American children.

Teacher effectiveness is crucial in ensuring equitable teaching methods. The quality of education students receive is determined by the influence of teacher efficacy. Instructors directly influence all aspects of students' learning (Linton, 2011; Sandoval et al., 2011; Stembridge, 2020). Furthermore, teachers who believe in their capacity to positively influence learning are likelier to engage African American children. They encourage them to participate and support them in overcoming academic obstacles. Educators with strong positive self-efficacy can bridge the educational gap for African American children. They do not set limits but raise the expectations for themselves and the children they encounter.

Teacher effectiveness can positively or negatively affect the ability to deliver equitable teaching. The teacher's everyday routines in the classroom require them to manage several obligations, which might lead to feeling overwhelmed, contributing to self-efficacy concerns. Teacher efficacy impacts student academic performance and endeavors to address the success disparity frequently noticed in racially and economically divided schools (Anderson & Olivier, 2022).

There are many educators who are uncertain about their ability to significantly impact students' academic advancement because of self-efficacy issues. These educators see everything as an obstacle. They never see the possibilities of the students. They only see the limitation. Students are never expected to excel academically.

Notable subject matter experts concur that teacher efficacy can significantly enhance student accomplishment. Educators exhibiting a robust sense of efficacy maintain elevated expectations for their students, as they possess a steadfast belief in their students' capacity for achievement (Bruce et al., 2010; Chism, 2022; Linton, 2011; Sandoval et al., 2011; Stembridge, 2020). These educators give additional time and focus to children that are underperforming. The collective beliefs of the instructors indicate that they may influence student accomplishment irrespective of the student's circumstances. The educators appreciate the academic uniqueness of the students they encounter. They regard the students positively, embracing their differences while addressing the educational shortfall. These educators see the light in their students and are willing to provide them with what they need to shine bright despite societal inequities.

Enhancing performance among staff members, both individually and collectively, is an essential element of educational equity. To promote equity, educators must be persuaded that they can improve children's achievement of educational equity. Educators who offer outstanding support to students instill confidence in the learners (Chism, 2022; Linton, 2011; Stembridge, 2020). This confidence is seen in the classroom and on standardized exams when the achievement gap reduces.

There is a deficit of teacher efficacy in many urban school districts. A. Evans (2009) stated that school personnel may lack confidence in the student's ability to achieve academic success and that "Inevitably, race, class, and the school's social environment affect the academic content and skills teachers choose to teach and their beliefs about students' ability to learn, as well as a belief about their ability to improve student's performance" (p. 66). For many teachers, a lack of self-esteem impacts their ability to teach effectively and provide equitable education. Chism (2022) stated that when walking through the hallways of a struggling school, it is possible to pick up on the tone of exhaustion and defeat from educators charged to raise the achievement of students of color.

Because of the testing requirements imposed by federal and state mandates, educators experience tremendous stress, which impacts their self-efficacy. Many educators focus on meeting the mandate and not the academic needs of the students. There are some teachers who aim to accomplish two objectives when providing educational justice. They equipped students for real-life situations or an examination. This can result in diminished self-efficacy of the teachers. When there are lower self-efficacy issues, African American children are at risk of receiving a sub-par education. There are several researchers who have looked at bias and teacher efficacy. They are Chism, 2022; Chu, 2019; Linton, 2011; Sandoval et al., 2011; Stembridge, 2020.

By tackling teacher efficacy and biases, educational institutions can strive for a more equitable educational environment. Teacher self-efficacy and bias are essential factors that influence the educational experiences and outcomes of African American children. Teachers' perceptions of their effectiveness affect their educational approaches and interactions with children. Elevated self-efficacy frequently correlates with more inclusive, supportive, and engaging educational settings. Thus, both explicit and implicit biases further intensify these issues. Unconscious biases or negative stereotypes held by teachers regarding African American children manifest in subtle yet pervasive manners. These practices may foster a cycle of underperformance, disconnection, and disengagement from the educational system.

Addressing these concerns enhances teacher practices and ensures educational equity for African American children. Educational justice eliminates all obstacles to providing children with equitable possibilities for success. This cannot occur if the educators who operate the system lack a robust sense of effectiveness or are unprepared to identify and confront their biases.

Where Do We Go from Here

Conscious or unconscious biases have deeply influenced the educational experience of African American children. It has created barriers that hinder academic and personal growth. The impact of these biases is pervasive. It affects everything from teacher expectations, disciplinary actions, curriculum choices, and allocation of resources. As a result, African American children often find themselves navigating a system that underestimates their potential but perpetuates inequity and exclusion. Addressing these biases requires more than just acknowledging their existence. It demands a comprehensive approach by reexamining institutional policies, cultivating culturally responsive teaching practices, and fostering a school culture that affirms and values the identities and capabilities of African American children. In order to dismantle these systemic barriers, educators, policymakers, and stakeholders must commit to ongoing self-reflection and professional development. While confronting uncomfortable truths about how biases shape educational outcomes.

Where do we go from here? Achieving educational justice for African American children involves multifaceted strategies. Urban schools must adopt anti-racist curriculum that challenge stereotypes and provide a more inclusive narrative. Teachers and administrators must engage in training to recognize and counteract biases. Furthermore, policies at the district, state, and federal levels must prioritize equity by providing resources, support, and opportunities. The journey to educational justice is not a solitary effort. Collaboration among educators, parents, students, and stakeholders is required to create an environment where African American children are empowered to succeed. In essence, educational justice means turning awareness into action, holding ourselves and our institutions accountable, and, most importantly, creating a future where the promise of education is fulfilled for every child, regardless of race or background.

CHAPTER 5: EQUITY AND INCLUSIVE PEDAGOGY FRAMEWORK (EIPF)

As an educator, I participate in professional development prior to the start of each academic year. The sessions attempt to equip educators and me with effective techniques to enhance teaching and learning. Certain workshops provided valuable tools. However, others were needless and seemed to create extra work without addressing the challenges that African American children face in the classroom regarding equitable instruction. These students encounter an academic disadvantage, needing Brown v. Board of Education mandates that provide equal educational opportunities. The systemic concerns created significant academic gaps within the equal education policy, therefore needing educational justice.

We operate within an educational context where African American children consistently encounter academic difficulties that inhibit them from obtaining educational justice. The COVID-19 pandemic increased the educational divide. A considerable percentage of children have already been negatively affected by systemic inequity and faced further challenges throughout the pandemic. The shift to virtual education limited access to needed resources and increased the achievement gap compared to their white peers. Many urban schools were unable to shift to online learning because of inadequate access to high-speed internet, computers, and suitable teaching environments. This impeded the children's capacity to participate in virtual learning and obtain a quality education. The repercussions of COVID-19 on education persist in urban schools. African American children are reading two to three grades below the expected level. A considerable number of students performed below grade level on state standardized tests. Consequently, mandating school districts to devise methods to bridge the academic gap.

Some scholars have suggested that to achieve and maintain educational justice, there needs to be a fundamental change in the approach to teaching (Chism, 2022; Elmore, 2008; A. Evans, 2009; Linton, 2011; Stembridge, 2020). Instead of providing the same instruction to all students, the focus should be on providing instruction tailored to each student's individual learning needs. This can be done by emphasizing the content and engagement of the instruction and by incorporating culturally relevant teaching methods. This viewpoint is supported by the works of Elmore (2008), Ladson-Billings (2009), Linton (2011), and Stembridge (2020).

While working on my dissertation, I developed a framework based on my research findings. Educators use strategies that developed the Equity and Inclusive Pedagogy Framework (EIPF) to provide educational justice. Genuine educational justice significantly influences teachers' actions and methods to ensure that every student, regardless of background or origin, may succeed (Linton, 2011; Stembridge, 2020). The research reflected the influence of equitable teaching methods on the learning outcomes of African American students. The research concepts established equitable practice and offered a roadmap for implementation. The EIPF assesses culture, curriculum, teacher/leader knowledge and skill, practice, and student outcomes. The replies from the focus group and survey participants unequivocally affirmed the significance of culture, topic, teacher expertise, and instructional strategies in influencing students' academic performance.

Figure 1
Equity and Inclusive Pedagogical Framework (EIPF)

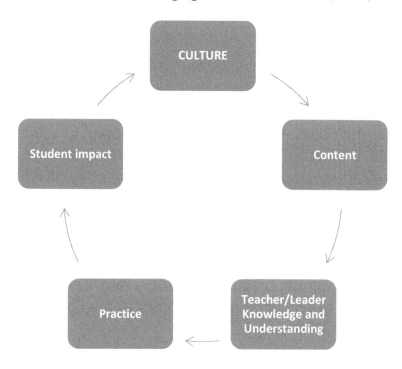

I designed this conceptual framework from my research

African American children need effective strategies to decrease the educational gap. Therefore, the Equity and Inclusive Pedagogy Framework (EIPF) can advance educational justice. An equity-focused pedagogy confronts systemic inequalities by recognizing the diverse needs of historically underserved children. EIPF ensures that resources, support, and opportunities are distributed based on individual needs rather than a blanket approach. It helps dismantle the barriers that perpetuate educational injustice. EIPF also integrates African American children's cultural backgrounds into the learning process. This helps the students see themselves reflected in the curriculum. Making learning more meaningful and fostering a sense of belonging. This would challenge Eurocentric narratives and help diversify the educational experience. This framework promotes justice by validating the experiences and histories of all students.

This framework focuses on educational justice because it aims to close the achievement gap for the disproportionately affected students of color. In order to support students' success, differentiated instruction is tailored to students to promote equitable academic outcomes. Inclusive pedagogy encourages the empowerment of the student's voice. It finds value in student input and encourages active participation. This helps African American children engage with a curriculum that affirms their identity and experience. Therefore, justice-based teaching encourages teachers and students to examine inequities in education. This encourages a generation of teachers, and students to advocate for social change and educational reform.

The components of the EIPF facilitate the transition of equity from theoretical concepts to practical implementation. Figure 1 demonstrates the necessity for education to transition from a focus on reality to a focus on justice. EIPF enables educators to tackle the disparities and obstacles that hinder the implementation of equitable teaching methods.

Culture

To attain educational equity for African American children, it is essential to examine culture from two viewpoints: a positive school culture and culturally responsive education (CRE). Culturally responsive education and a healthy school culture are essential for attaining educational equity for African American children. When educational practices, rules, and environments align with African American students' cultural experiences and identities, they foster equity, inclusivity, and academic achievement. The school's culture that embraces and respects all students' uniqueness fosters an academic atmosphere favorable to educational equity.

In various urban public schools, it is essential to recognize the cultural heritage of African American children within the curriculum. This enables children to recognize themselves and their background within the curriculum, cultivating a sense of pride and self-esteem. It also counters negative misconceptions that could otherwise prevail in mainstream narratives, thus undermining African American children's self-esteem and sense of belonging. Advocating for educational justice guarantees all children access to superior resources, opportunities, and equitable treatment. This facilitates the closure of the achievement gap and empowers African American children to realize their full potential.

The implementation of culturally responsive education supports educational justice. This approach recognizes and utilizes students' cultural backgrounds, experiences, and learning styles, which is an asset to their educational process. Culturally relevant education addresses inequities by enhancing academic engagement and performance. This education style reflects African American experiences and allows for a more comprehensive development of students. It helps them navigate a world with a stronger sense of identity and critical thinking skills necessary to challenge societal injustices. When African American children learn about their culture, history, and struggles for justice, they are empowered to advocate for themselves and their community. Ensuring African American children have access to an equitable, culturally aware education breaks the intergenerational cycle of inequality.

Culturally responsive education moves away from a deficit-based perspective that frames African American children and their community as insufficient. Instead, it recognizes and builds on the cultural capital and strengths they bring to the classroom. This approach reframes the perception of African American children's inabilities and looks at their abilities. Furthermore, this leads to a shift in educators' expectations and interactions with these children.

School culture refers to the norms, values, practices, and policies that shape a school's social and academic environment. A positive, inclusive school culture is critical for achieving educational justice for African American children. Bayar and Karaduman (2021) assert that school culture is vital in setting standards and defining objectives to be attained. Celikten (2006) suggested that school culture comprises individuals' shared ideals, behaviors, and beliefs inside a school. Consequently, the school's culture can influence the equitable instructional techniques afforded to African American students.

A comprehensive understanding of a school's culture is crucial for enhancing its effectiveness for children (Bayar & Karaduman, 2021). A welcoming and inclusive school culture fosters a sense of belonging. Schools that celebrate diversity host culturally relevant events and promote inclusion, creating spaces where children feel safe and valued. Bayar and Karaduman (2021) asserted that school culture influences the development of individual personalities throughout time, similar to the uniqueness of each person's character. Furthermore, Bayar and Karaduman assert that the ideals of schools and the personalities of staff members, students, and parents are critical elements in the formation of school culture.

As Bayar and Karaduman (2021) stated, school leaders must establish a strong and favorable school culture. Based on Linton (2011), a strong learning culture in a school creates an environment where teachers, leaders, and students feel encouraged to take chances, challenge themselves, and learn without apprehension. Providing an equitable education will benefit African American children in this conducive setting. An inclusive school climate reduces the likelihood of exclusionary practices. Therefore, African American students will not feel culturally alienated or remain silent, which is a common experience (DeCuir & Dixson, 2004).

Schools with a culturally responsive climate prioritize building strong, trusting relationships between students and teachers. These relationships are crucial for African American children. Many of these students face implicit biases and stereotypes that hinder positive student-teacher dynamics. Teachers who understand and appreciate the children's cultural background in their schools are better equipped to interact with African American children. Therefore, culturally competent educators learn about themselves first (Aguilar, 2020; Linton, 2011). They address their biases, beliefs, and judgments regarding students who do not look like them or come from the same socioeconomic status. Aguilar (2020) and Linton (2011) further stated that culturally competent teachers understand their students according to race, culture, ethnicity, background, and learning needs. According to Aguilar and Linton, this is the remedy for equitable practices.

Elmore (2008) noted that "Most low-performing schools do not need more programs or even more resources. They need a more powerful, coherent culture of instructional practice" (p. 2). Most researchers agree that all individuals involved in education should prioritize the development of educators' learning cultures and cultural competencies (Aguilar, 2020; Elmore, 2008; Linton, 2011). Prioritizing this development is crucial in bridging the divide between instructors and students from different cultural backgrounds. Bayar and Karaduman (2021) stated that school culture has a favorable impact on student accomplishment and motivation and on teacher productivity and satisfaction. Their research further demonstrated that school culture substantially impacts student motivation and academic performance. Linton (2011) and Chism (2022) also found that culture is essential to the equity puzzle.

It is imperative that we teach African American children using methods that value their thinking and speaking or that respect their lived experience. EIPF prioritizes culture as its primary priority. This includes implementing culturally responsive education (CRE) and linking classroom culture and climate. Educators should cultivate culture via teaching, recognize the need to establish a secure and inclusive learning atmosphere, foster connections, and possess knowledge about the diverse student population they face in their classes.

EIPF has a profound impact on the educational culture and experience of African American children. Properly implementing this framework can transform schools into environments that acknowledge, celebrate, and nurture these children's unique identities and learning needs. The school culture and the culturally responsive practices of the educational stakeholders promote a sense of identity by countering the historical marginalization of African American children. EIPF uses school culture and culturally relevant practices to address different learning styles, which helps close achievement gaps.

By aligning EIPF educational practices with the needs and experiences of African American children, culture and culturally responsive education are vital in dismantling systemic barriers and achieving educational justice for African American children. This type of combination has been shown to reduce achievement gaps by promoting higher academic expectations. It allows students to engage in meaningful learning, reduces inequities, and promotes upward social mobility.

Culturally responsive education and a positive school culture are essential to educational justice for African American children. Implementing culturally affirming practices creates physical and psychological safe spaces for African American children. School culture and culturally responsive education ensure the educational environment is affirming, inclusive, and equitable. Furthermore, it addresses historical and present-day disparities. Schools that embrace these approaches support African American children's academic and personal success and contribute to transforming the educational system to be more just and reflective of all students' experiences.

Content

Many students struggled to connect to the academic content in my early teaching stages. The stories in the textbooks and novels were unrelatable to the African American children reading them. Therefore, it was extremely hard for the children to engage with instruction. This was a major issue because the children were not reaching the proficiency goal on state standardized tests. The content the children were exposed to continues to widen the educational gap. Therefore, educational content is crucial to the education of African American children. Content shapes their learning experience, identity, and sense of belonging.

When considering the importance of educational content for African American children, I looked at the work Elmore, Ladson-Billing, Linton, and Stembridge had completed to improve equitable instructional practice. Each individual examined the importance of educational content and its impact on students' learning. Their frameworks and theories address various aspects of education, from instructional quality to cultural responsiveness and systemic change. By addressing instructional practices, content relevance, systemic inequities, and inclusivity, these scholars offer a multi-faceted approach to promoting educational justice. This ensures that African American children have equitable academic and social opportunities within the educational system.

As educators, it is important that we use content that students can connect with by dismantling inequities that hinder the academic success of African American children. In our urban schools, children should be exposed to content that includes diverse characters and cultural references that allow connections to their identities and reference relatable experiences and stories that matter. Incorporating rich and affirming content in African American children's educational experience is essential in a diverse school experience. This approach disrupts biases and stereotypes. The ultimate goal is for the children to see themselves positively in their education.

The equity and inclusion pedagogy framework (EIPF) significantly influences the content and delivery of education for African American children (Thomas-Jones, 2024). The framework aims to ensure that educational practices are equitable and responsive. Education content within EIPF prioritizes how it fosters identity, belonging, and pride. The content shifts how the students are represented but provides a roadmap to dismantle structural inequities that hinder the academic success of African American children. Equipping African American children with the tools to achieve their full potential. It seeks to build an equitable learning environment through collaboration and eliminating the educational gap.

Therefore, the second component of EIPF is the content or material presented to students. The curriculum should be tailored to accommodate the specific requirements and preferences of the students. It should be culturally responsive education. According to Linton (2011), students require educational assistance that differs from many schools' uniform treatment. My research revealed that exposing students to various content that fully captured equitable practices helped them succeed academically.

Many African American children in urban schools are exposed to outdated material with limited diversity. This content prevents the children from engaging in content that allows them to be empathetic with diverse ideas and perspectives. In this educational content, African American children are not displayed as resilient or respectful of diverse cultures and harmful stereotypes. The EIPF requires that educational content foster a deep respect for African American children's culture and eliminate harmful stereotypes (Thomas-Jones, 2024). EIPF looks at content holistically by including diverse narratives that encourage all children. The content provides equity and social responsibility, allowing African American children to be resilient and excel (Thomas-Jones, 2024). The content should be challenging and culturally affirming by empowering

African American children to succeed through tailored support and inclusive practices.

Content is fundamentally important to equitable instruction and is essential to educating African American children (City et al., 2009; Elmore, 2008). It serves as the medium where teachers help students access skills, knowledge, and educational perspectives. As Elmore (2008) wrote, "Increases in student learning occur only as a consequence of improvements in the level of content, teachers' knowledge and skill, and student engagement" (p. 2). Content address educational inequalities by providing students with rigorous but equitable instruction (Stembridge, 2020). This approach helps African American children bridge the academic gap.

Content fosters equitable and significant possibilities for students to engage in a holistic learning environment. This diverse content allows for deeper development of African American children's abilities for deep thinking and practical actions (Elmore, 2008; Stembridge, 2020). Equitable instruction requires content to be tailored and readily available to students with different skill levels to meet their individual learning styles. The academic content that African American children are exposed to can challenge or reinforce existing power dynamics and systemic inequities. Moreover, content should be designed from an equity lens (Linton, 2011). Content can reinforce existing inequities or bridge gaps that foster an equitable learning environment for students.

Equitable teaching methods guarantee that material is available to all students (City et al., 2009; Elmore, 2008; Linton, 2011) and that it is tailored to fit the needs and learning styles of underprivileged students (Chism, 2022; Stembridge, 2020; Thomas-Jones, 2024). It is shown in several inclusive ways that expose children to varied instruction, and culturally relevant content allows them to enhance their learning and close the academic learning gap (Santangelo & Tomlinson, 2012; Stembridge, 2020). Therefore, the materials teachers expose their students to, should provide equitable opportunities for them to flourish academically. The content given to African American children must be diverse, accessible, and culturally relevant, which, as a top priority, helps to provide equitable learning environments. When materials encourage participation, students can flourish in an equitable classroom.

The content presented to African American children in schools profoundly impacts their journey toward educational justice. Curriculums that lack representation, omit significant cultural contributions, or perpetuate stereotypes that serve as barriers hindering not only academic achievement but also the holistic development of these students. When African American children encounter an education system that diminishes or negates their identities and histories, it reinforces a sense of marginalization and disconnect from their learning.

Achieving educational justice requires educators and stakeholders to use transformative content that reflects the rich diversity, complexity, and resilience of the African American experience. EIPF can create a sense of belonging, build self-efficacy, and empower African American children to see themselves as active participants in their educational journey. This is a necessary step toward correcting historical inequities. It shifts to including and creating a learning environment where all children can thrive. By restricting educational content, we lay the groundwork for the educational justice landscape. This paves the way for an educational system that supports African American children and brings them closer to educational justice.

Teacher/Leader Knowledge and Understanding

In many school districts, there is a huge disparity between the ethnicity of the teachers and students. That can cause a disconnect between teachers and African American children. In high school, there wasn't an African American teacher or staff member in the building. There was no connection between educators and students. I felt like I was misunderstood trying to get an education because there was no staff I could relate to or seek out help when I experienced microaggressions. If I can feel this way, imagine other children in urban school districts taught by educators who cannot relate to them. Teachers with inadequate knowledge of African American culture may unknowingly and knowingly perpetuate stereotypes or hold implicit biases that impact their expectations and interactions with students.

Therefore, teachers with a deep knowledge and understanding of African American history, culture, and experiences are better equipped to create culturally responsive and relevant instruction. These educators are more likely to approach teaching with an equity mindset because they are educated on African American children's historical and systemic challenges. They address biases and promote a positive educational environment for students. Furthermore, teachers who are knowledgeable about educational inequities are better prepared to challenge inequitable practices and policies within schools and advocate for students.

Teachers are essential to the instructional core as they bring knowledge and skills to the classroom. In many school districts, educators spend most of their time venting about the challenges of education and not the possibilities of empowering students to achieve academically. Within the scope of Linton's (2011) equity framework, "Educators provide all students with the individual support they need to reach and exceed goals" (p. 39). Therefore, teacher knowledge and understanding are critical components in the Equity and Inclusive Pedagogy Framework (EIPF). Offering African American children educational justice.

The third component of EIPF pertains to the knowledge and expertise teachers and leaders possess. The educator or leader acknowledges and confronts personal prejudices that may influence their teaching. Barnes (2021) explicitly acknowledges the presence of unconscious prejudice in individuals, which impacts the educational setting for students from varied backgrounds. In my research, educators acknowledged their prejudices and took steps to ensure that these biases did not impact their interactions with their students. Within the EIPF, educators and administrators cater to individual student's abilities and refrain from delivering uniform content to all students. Educators and administrators often transcend superficial equity to meet basic curriculum needs. An equitable educational environment is created when educators use effective techniques to include students in academic activities. These activities allow for student engagement at their academic level. These educators understand the lived experience of African American children and build trust and rapport. These are the foundations for better academic and social outcomes.

Teachers acquire and employ equitable teaching methods by establishing a strong link between theoretical knowledge, practical application, and active participation in social interactions (Lotan, 2006). If students in high-poverty schools have less equipped instructors to teach core subjects, these teachers would also lack the ability to address the numerous social and psychological concerns commonly observed in impoverished students (Anderson & Olivier, 2022). Teachers facilitate students' development of self-regulation skills and enhance their comprehension of the targeted academic ideas. According to Bruce et al. (2010), students in classrooms where teachers have high teacher efficacy exhibit improved study habits. Teacher direction, student determination, deep conceptual comprehension, and self-regulation, all cultivated in high-effectiveness classrooms, are key factors that contribute to students enhanced academic performance.

Effective educators not only establish objectives for themselves but also establish objectives for their students and maintain high expectations for them. They are confident in enhancing student learning by going above and beyond and using effective teaching methods to achieve educational justice. These educators have high expectations and provide relevant and affirming learning experiences. Therefore, African American children are more likely to achieve at higher levels and remain engaged in their education. Teachers with demonstrated expertise in their subject areas can produce more significant outcomes with their students.

Moreover, educators' expertise and understanding are crucial in influencing African American children's educational experiences and outcomes. The efficacy of educational justice efforts depends on instructors' capacity to connect with students as learners and individuals. Educators have a profound comprehension that customizes their instructional methods to address the specific demands of African American pupils. The expertise and comprehension of educators cultivate an inclusive and supportive learning atmosphere.

Ultimately, EIPF attains educational equity for African American children not merely by enacting changes but through the methods employed by educators. Informed educators are pivotal in challenging inequitable trends and bridging gaps in education. These educators eliminate obstacles and foster a profound understanding of the African American children present in the classroom. Providing these children with the opportunity to be acknowledged and respected.

Practice

In urban schools, educators frequently highlight students' deficiencies without scrutinizing their own practices and their effects on student learning. This renders students powerless and disconnected from the educational process, exacerbating the educational gap. Dr. Mary McLeod Bethune advocates for educators and stakeholders to perceive students as unrefined diamonds requiring guidance and empowerment to thrive. Education serves as a mechanism for achieving justice for African American children. Nevertheless, the school system for numerous African American children has evolved into a pathway to incarceration. Not enough consideration is afforded to enhancing teachers' self-efficacy to improve their practice and knowledge to empower African American children.

Teacher practice is pivotal for African American children to achieve educational justice. An equity-centered approach to teaching intentionally addresses educational gaps and limitations within the classroom. Effective teachers practice actively differentiated instruction, employ culturally relevant teaching, and provide resources to support the needs of African American children. This ensures that all students have equitable opportunities to succeed, resulting in meaningful outcomes for African American children. When teachers' practices relate to the students, they are more likely to build meaningful relationships. They interact more with the lessons, and teachers know to navigate students learning more effectively.

The subsequent element of the EIPF is practice. Educators employ several methodologies that foster equity and offer assistance and direction. My research revealed that teacher instructional design plays a major role in equitable instructional practices. The educators who participated in my study indicated that instructors should establish a secure setting for students, fostering their comfort and granting them autonomy in guiding their own learning, thereby promoting a liberating atmosphere (Thomas-Jones, 2024). These results are connected to educators' practices. Therefore, teachers must take significant responsibility for their practice and implement strategies to be effective in the classroom. They must also ensure that their practices and knowledge are tailored to the student's needs by implementing instructional techniques that employ differentiated instruction and culturally relevant education for African American children. These practices offer diverse instructional activities while maintaining consistent materials and catering to all learners' needs in the classroom (Hedrick, 2012; Kanevsky, 2011; Stembridge, 2020; Tomlinson, 1999; Thomas-Jones, 2024; Williams, 2023).

Linton (2011) observed, "The practice strategy emphasizes the daily actions of teachers in the classroom and their influence on student achievement" (p. 61). Moreover, how educators interact with and engage their students might alter the educational trajectory among these children. They are deliberate in their pedagogical approaches due to their confidence in the kids they engage with. Competent educators do not permit the obstacles of their personal experiences to influence their academic preparation of students. To develop effective pedagogical methods and enhance capacity, educators must recognize the cultures experienced by students and cultivate abilities to facilitate their learning (Linton, 2011). Effective educators skillfully teach children and bridge the educational divide for African American children. Moreover, effective instruction is enhanced by a strong culture and effective leadership (Chism, 2022; Linton, 2011; Stembridge, 2020). Educators are diligent in their application of EIPF as it utilizes effective strategies.

In education, teachers feel that their practice in the classroom is impacted by increased emphasis on testing and the dependency on scripted curriculum, and the school climate impacts instructional practices (DiCicco et al., 2016). Educators must refrain from allowing the cultural backgrounds of the students they teach to impact their practice and assessment of the intellectual capacity of these children, especially those from disadvantaged socioeconomic backgrounds and ethnic minorities (Colgren & Sappington, 2015). Teachers should acknowledge and appreciate the significant contributions made by all students, especially those from low-income backgrounds and minority groups. This understanding should be used to establish equitable chances for all children to thrive academically and in their future endeavors.

Effective teaching practice occurs when sound pedagogy is present (Linton, 2011). Hence, educators recognizing and capitalizing on students' existing abilities while recognizing areas where they may be lacking is a commendable approach to attaining equitable treatment (Dack et al., 2022). Teachers should demonstrate a willingness to thoroughly examine every aspect of their teaching methods to guarantee they implement equitable procedures. Effective instruction starts with a well-defined vision and a solid objective (Linton, 2011; Stembridge, 2020). Prioritizing plans to practice equity acknowledges the objective of fostering student involvement and comprehension (Stembridge, 2020).

The integration of pedagogy, cultural competence, and equitable practices determines whether classrooms serve as environments that promote educational liberty or perpetuate marginalization. When educators adopt a culturally responsive approach to their teaching practices, they recognize the distinct problems and capabilities that African American children contribute to the classroom. Many traditional teaching techniques frequently exhibit biases and deficit thinking that disproportionately disadvantage African American children. These practices result in diminished academic expectations and restricted possibilities for advanced placement classes. Consequently, altering teacher practices goes beyond mere instructional improvement. This is a crucial factor for achieving educational justice.

Instructional methods must evolve accordingly to achieve genuine educational justice. This entails implementing an asset-based strategy, the Equity and Inclusive Pedagogy Framework (EIPF). Educators utilizing EIPF can eliminate the academic obstacles that contribute to educational gaps. Teachers' practices build equitable learning environments where African American children feel respected, supported, and empowered to achieve their greatest potential. Ultimately, pursuing educational justice requires a shared effort from educators, administrators, and policymakers to reevaluate and reform the education structure by prioritizing the voices, experiences, and aspirations of African American children in educational practices. This enables educators and stakeholders to advance toward a genuinely equitable and inclusive educational system for all African American children.

Student Impact

Whitney Houston's song, The *Greatest Love of All, resonates deeply, particularly* with its powerful line, "I believe the children are the future. Teach them well and let them lead the way." Many African American children sang these words for generations, fueled by the belief that they could achieve anything with a strong education. In 2024, despite ongoing efforts from educators and stakeholders, a persistent achievement gap remains, with African American students continuing to lag behind their White peers. Systemic inequities have consistently impeded their progress. Many urban districts make frequent curriculum adjustments to improve outcomes, but these changes remain insufficient. Therefore, these children long to be taught well so they can lead the way in society. So, achieving true educational justice requires more than surface-level modification. It demands a commitment to dismantling the deeper, structural barriers that hinder African American children's academic success.

Educators, curriculum, and stakeholders must adopt an inclusive strategy to enhance students' involvement. When the academic curriculum includes African American experiences and recognizes students as co-creators of knowledge, it fosters diverse perspectives essential for achieving educational justice. The influence of student outcomes guides the choice of educational resources, classroom dialogues, and methods of instruction. This guarantees that all students feel included and represented. Even well-meaning instructional methods might perpetuate inequalities when students' perspectives are unrepresented. As a result, in the EIPF, student impact is a crucial element, especially in the pursuit of educational equity.

The EIPF impacts student perspectives and enhances the educational gaps African American children face. This enables the student to take ownership of their education. Teacher and student interaction is seamless in an effective classroom that empowers rather than degrades African American children. In my research, the teacher openly stated that treating children with respect, employing a culturally relevant curriculum, and permitting students to engage in exploratory learning yields positive outcomes for students. The participants reported an improvement in both informative and formative evaluation. Therefore, the impact of educational practices on students directly influences how equity is measured. Educational justice demands a commitment to adjusting our academic approach based on student impact.

Furthermore, Elmore (2008) and Linton (2011) are two researchers who also examined the impact of student engagement. In their work, they identified that students positively receive deeper learning when actively engaging in their learning process. Therefore, EIPF connects to the instructional core and equity framework. These three frameworks focus on instructional practices and engagement that invest in students behaviorally, effectively, and/or cognitively. EIPF results and performance drive students and how they respond to equitable instructional practices.

EIPF, like the other educational frameworks, assigns accountability to students. Students must work to achieve educational equity by engaging with their learning. When structures are in place like EIPF, it supports all aspects of students' education and development. Student performance can be linked to the school's culture and teacher interaction. When students identify with a healthy school culture, they establish relationships with staff, teachers, and administrators because relationships matter (Cook et al., 2016; Elmore, 2008; Linton, 2011; Thomas-Jones, 2024).

Student engagement is essential to achieving equitable practices (Chism, 2022; Chu, 2019; Elmore, 2008; Linton, 2011; Stembridge, 2020). True engagement goes beyond participation. It includes making children feel that they are supported and valued in their learning community. Chism's (2022) work on equity emphasized that when teachers understand and connect with their students, it strengthens students' identities and fosters both academic and social engagement. This engagement, in turn, builds critical thinking skills and motivates students to take on challenging assignments. According to City et al. (2009), students should be interested and actively involved in assignments and able to explain and reflect on what they are learning. By fostering such engagement, educators help African American children reach their full potential, which advances educational justice.

Differentiated instruction is a powerful tool to further support this engagement and commitment to equity. When educators tailor lessons to meet each student's individual learning styles, readiness, and interest. This creates an inclusive and impactful learning environment, ensuring that all students can fully participate and succeed. Therefore, researchers (Hedrick, 2012; Ismajli & Imami-Morina, 2018; Kanevsky, 2011; Santangelo & Tomlinson, 2012; Williams, 2023), agree that this strategy can improve students' academic performance and provide equity. Teachers carefully design different instruction levels to meet students' needs and enhance student engagement.

Differentiated instruction, as an approach to advancing educational justice, enables teachers to meet the needs of diverse learners. It creates a collaborative relationship between teachers and students. This builds trust and closes the academic gaps for students in urban districts. Through customized teaching instruction, differentiated instruction promotes educational justice by ensuring equitable access to rigorous academic content for all students. By adapting lessons to meet the needs of African American children, teachers see improvements in academic growth. This strategy maintains high academic standards and challenges students to excel while making learning accessible and relevant (DiCicco et al., 2016; Kanevsky, 2011; Santangelo & Tomlinson, 2012; VanTassel-Baska & Stambaugh, 2005; Williams, 2023).

To realize the full potential of differentiated instruction, it is essential to address barriers. Insufficient professional development leaves many educators without the strategies or confidence to implement effective differentiation. There are underfunded school districts, classes with limited resources, and a high student-to-teacher ratio makes personalized teaching a challenge. Schools can address these obstacles by investing in professional development tailored to differentiated instruction, curriculum modifications, alternative assessment, and classroom management. By tackling these challenges, differentiated instruction can be an effective tool for achieving educational justice. The main goal is to ensure that all students receive a quality education.

If an educator has difficulties with efficacy and bias regarding equitable instructional practices, it will impact student engagement. The educators will be unable to address students' social and emotional needs. The learning environment where educators are intimidated limits students' engagement. However, when teachers feel confident in their abilities and empowered to foster a positive learning environment, this can profoundly impact student achievement, motivation, and engagement.

Teachers with high self-efficacy set higher expectations for their students. They can provide better feedback and are more likely to use effective instructional strategies. When teachers believe in their capacity to influence African American children, they create a classroom climate that encourages risk-taking, collaboration, and intellectual curiosity. This increases students' motivation and engagement, which is crucial for long-term academic success. Teachers with high self-efficacy are likely to embrace diverse instructional methods to reach learners. They are better equipped to address students' needs and do not employ deficit student narratives. Instead, they focus on their ability to make a difference, leading to more equitable expectations and teaching practices.

Equipping African American children with equitable access to high-quality education marks systematic advancement toward educational equity. Student impact can expose how well policies, instructional strategies, and community involvement initiatives support an inclusive and encouraging classroom. The differences in student results often draw attention to current inequities in institutional support, resources, and opportunities. Reaching educational equity depends on addressing these differences. EIPF gives techniques that make students' different needs and experiences a top priority. Thus, EIPF can be used by teachers and other stakeholders to help to reduce the consequences of inequalities and create an atmosphere where African American children may flourish. This strategy guarantees that educational fairness is not only a theoretical idea, but a practical reality shown in the lives of African American children.

Furthermore, the impact of African American children's outcomes extends beyond individual success. It serves as a crucial benchmark for educational systems. Schools that embrace equitable practices and focus on positive student outcomes contribute to the broader social mission of reducing educational inequalities and promoting social justice. The pursuit of educational justice is not only about rectifying past injustices. It's about building a future where African American children are empowered to reach their full potential. African American students who are prepared academically will transform communities and society at large.

We do not need a Band-Aid. We Want Educational Justice

Equity and inclusive pedagogy framework (EIPF) are more than another educational strategy buzzword. It is a transformative approach that can reshape the learning experience of African American children and foster an environment where all students are valued and supported (Thomas-Jones, 2024). Implementing this framework goes beyond superficial fixes. It requires a fundamental rethinking of how we view teaching, learning, and the role of education in addressing historical and contemporary injustice.

Equity-driven and inclusive pedagogy has a profound impact on African American children. When classrooms become spaces that honor diverse perspectives, celebrate cultural backgrounds, and promote critical thinking, students are more engaged, confident, and better positioned to achieve

130

academic success. Inclusive pedagogies challenge deficit-based narratives and disrupt the low expectations that have historically marginalized African American children. By creating a curriculum that reflects their identities, experiences, and contributions, we affirm the dignity and potential of every child.

However, to truly achieve educational justice, we cannot settle for quick fixes or temporary interventions. Band-aid solutions that address surface-level symptoms of inequity without confronting the underlying structures of oppression will continue to perpetuate disparities in achievement and opportunity. Educational justice demands a comprehensive and sustained commitment to equity. Inclusive pedagogy is not an add-on but a core principle guiding educational practices.

Educational justice begins with embracing discomfort and committing to transformative change. Urban schools must integrate equity and inclusivity into their operations, from classroom instructions and assessment to hiring practices and community engagement. Policymakers must invest in policies that support educators in adopting these frameworks and hold institutions accountable for outcomes. Most importantly, the voices of African American children and their communities must be at the forefront of these efforts. Ensuring the systems to serve African American children are designed with their needs and aspirations in mind is necessary. However, EIPF, is a tool that can be used to improve educators and student engagement.

Achieving educational justice means rejecting the temptation of a band-aid solution. There is a need to pursue genuine systemic change. It means creating learning environments where African American children can thrive without having to navigate the constraints of bias, exclusion, or systemic barriers. We can center equity and inclusive pedagogy as foundational elements in our education system only when we dismantle the legacy of educational inequity and build a future where justice prevails for every child.

CHAPTER 6: THE ROAD TO JUSTICE

In the year 2024, we are faced with book bands, Critical Race Theory legitimation, whether slavery was voluntary or involuntary, the discontinuation of affirmative action, the possible elimination of diversity, equity, and inclusion, and the continued decline in educational equity for African American children. Therefore, the road to educational justice continues to be very bumpy. The educational systems take three steps forward and twenty steps backward as time progresses. As an educator, it is very bothersome that a system that was developed to empower continues to be crippled by the systematic bureaucracy.

James Baldwin wrote it was expected of Black people to make peace with mediocracy because societal expectations were that they were worthless and not expected to achieve much. We live in a time when moderate progress was made to improve a flawed system. Even though years have gone by, and laws and regulations continue to be put in place to improve a system that allowed the educational disadvantage for African American children, there are still inequities that exist. The journey forward for African American children forever evolves because the bar is constantly set higher each year with little help to improve the educational gap. The time is now to implement strategies to improve this flawed system.

Past

In the past, African Americans were dehumanized by a society that had minimal expectations. The only aspiration was that this marginalized group would work for a set number of years to gain freedom and possibly acquire land or resources to establish themselves. As the demand for labor grew, Africans increasingly faced racial discrimination and systemic legal changes that gradually denied them rights. The expectations shifted from participating freely in society to a status of enslavement based on race.

African Americans were primarily viewed and expected to serve as laborers, working on plantations, in households, and other forms of manual labor. Their status was reduced to property, with no legal rights or recognition of humanity. African American people had to submit and acquiesce to White Americans. Enslaved people were denied education, personal freedom, and the right to a familial or community bond. Leaving African Americans to be marginalized by a system that was designed to treat them as inferior.

With the expectations set for African American people, education was not a priority. Therefore, when times and laws began to change, African American children started at an academic deficit because they were prohibited from learning how to read or receiving any form of education. When laws were finally instituted to educate African American children, many of the parents were illiterate and could not help with schoolwork. Therefore, an entire family has limited knowledge and resources to navigate an educational system.

Furthermore, Figure 3. shows that educational laws require that African American children receive an equal education. This would have been acceptable if the educational playing field was equal from the first day Africans arrived in this country. However, history has shown that it was not until the late 1950s that laws were established that required African American children to receive an education. The education system was plagued with many disparities and limitations. Despite educational and legal advancement, African Americans continued to face systemic inequalities in education. Therefore, past educational experiences have consistently failed to provide educational justice. Segregation, legal and de facto, placed African American children at a significant disadvantage compared to their White peers.

Figure 2: Equality

Image Credit: @restoringracialjustice

African Americans achieved some progress with an equal educational system. Nonetheless, systemic difficulties persistently hinder the intellectual advancement of African

American children. If education were genuinely fair, African American children would be able to compete academically. These children would have been sufficiently equipped to engage in the workforce and excel in higher education. Moreover, the inadequate equal system leads to disproportionate academic outcomes among racial groupings.

These previous educational experiences were attributed to insufficient resources and ineffective policymaking. It was founded on a tradition of prejudice based on race and an absence of genuine commitment to equity and justice. Consequently, African American children were deprived of educational justice. This had a profound effect on subsequent generations. There were barriers to social, economic, and intellectual advancement. Addressing this past necessitates recognizing centuries of these shortcomings. Deconstructing the frameworks that sustain educational disparities. This would ensure that African American students have a future dedicated to educational equity, a real reality.

I do not wish to undermine the equal system and its influence on the education of African American children. Despite the challenges afflicting urban areas, the village united and promoted education as the path to significant accomplishment. Regardless of the parent's educational background, they established an essential goal for their children to not only graduate from high school but also pursue higher education. The entire neighborhood rejoiced when a child from the inner city graduated from college. It instilled hope in others that they could achieve academic excellence. The past has facilitated the present environment in which African Americans can advocate for a system of justice and demand an education that addresses systemic challenges.

Present

Many educational practices and policies today are deeply rooted in the inequities of the past, hindering true progress. In 2024, it feels as though we're on the express train moving backward. Returning to the same one-sided education system that existed a century ago. This system was designed to benefit only a select few while leaving others with the bare minimum. Then and now, America's education system resembles Figure 4, where only certain groups receive educational advantages. While marginalized communities, particularly African American children, remain underserved. With the threat of Project 2025, the Department of Education will be dismantled, and that can cause further educational disparities.

Figure 3: Education Reality

Image Credit: @restoringracialjustice

Education has undergone numerous reforms, each promising to improve equity. African American children still face significant social, economic, and political disparities in education. Educational justice requires more than equal access to resources. It demands actively dismantling the biases and systemic barriers that have disadvantaged African American students from the beginning. This means building an education system that doesn't just acknowledge inequity but works tirelessly to eliminate it.

We've reached a point where African American children can no longer afford to rely solely on passive participants to lead the charge. Now, more than ever, we need true educational disruptors. Those who are ready to challenge the status quo and fight for change. These disruptors should be in classrooms, on school boards, in policymaking positions, and among families, speaking out with urgency and resolve. They understand that educational justice should not be the exception but the standard, and they are committed to making it a reality for every child.

Empowering Communities

Empowering communities to have an active voice in the education of African American children is a critical step toward achieving educational justice. Educational outcomes are not shaped solely within the walls of schools. They are influenced by the broader community in which children learn, grow, and develop. When communities are strengthened and given the resources to actively support their children's educational journey, they become powerful agents of change. They are capable of addressing systemic barriers and advocating for educational justice.

To provide an effective support structure, achieving educational equity for African American children involves a partnership approach, including families, educators, community leaders, and lawmakers. When school districts allocate resources to community-driven initiatives like mentorship programs, extracurricular activities, parental involvement, and culturally relevant education, it strengthens the community. With community assistance, African American children can establish a foundation fostering intellectual, social, and emotional growth. This form of community empowerment cultivates a sense of accountability. It guarantees that the perspectives of African American children are acknowledged and prioritized.

Moreover, when communities are empowered, they can advocate for policy changes. This allows resources to be allocated to address challenges facing African American children. Community members can push for culturally responsive curriculum, equitable funding, and inclusive school environments that celebrate diversity and promote belonging. Strong communities serve as buffers against external factors that negatively impact educational outcomes. Therefore, when we empower communities, it recognizes that African American children do not exist in isolation. The community realizes that the children's success is intertwined with the community's well-being. Educational systems respond kindly when communities advocate, support, and enrich the lives of African American children. This collaboration creates a just and equitable educational landscape for these children. The community center approach to educational justice acknowledges that social structures influence educational outcomes.

This includes involving parents and community leaders in decision-making processes related to curriculum design, school policies, and resource allocation. When communities are actively involved, schools are more likely to meet the needs of their students and promote positive educational outcomes.

Future

In 2024, there is a looming threat to achieving equitable education that may remain elusive. The fate of the Department of Education, whether it will persist or be abolished by Project 2025, hinges on the presidential election's outcome. Consequently, this can impede the attainment of educational equity for African American children. It is unrealistic to anticipate that these children will be able to compete in a society that must appropriately equip them.

Educational justice cannot be achieved by just one person. It takes all stakeholders. Educational stakeholders involved in establishing an equitable educational landscape include educators, school administrators, lawmakers, community leaders, and parents, all of whom have valuable roles to play. These stakeholders actively address inequities by recognizing that this is a fundamental step toward achieving educational justice for African American children.

Teachers and school staff are on the front lines of addressing inequities in the classroom. The standard curriculum often overlooks African American history and contribution, leading to a lack of engagement and a sense of alienation among students. Schools can make education more inclusive and affirming by implementing a culturally relevant curriculum. This can boost students' self-esteem while addressing their needs and challenging biases. Educators can create an inclusive environment where African American children can thrive.

Addressing inequities through professional development that includes anti-bias training and fostering a diverse teaching workforce can help ensure that African American students are treated fairly and that their cultural backgrounds are respected and valued.

Principals and other school leaders are responsible for implementing policies and practices that promote equity. By ensuring fair allocation of resources, supporting professional development focused on equity, and fostering a positive school culture, administrators can directly influence the educational experiences of African American students. By adopting restorative justice practices and creating a supportive, inclusive school climate, schools can reduce these disparities, ensuring that all students have the opportunity to succeed academically and socially.

Community organizations and leaders play a vital role in advocating for the needs of African American children. By partnering with schools, offering support services, and holding educational institutions accountable, community leaders help ensure that equity is a central focus in education.

Parents and guardians are key advocates for their children's education. By engaging in school activities, voicing concerns about inequities, and working with schools to ensure that their children receive a fair and equitable education, they contribute to the larger movement for educational justice. Schools that actively collaborate with parents and community organizations can better address the specific needs of African American students and create a more supportive and empowering educational environment.

When these stakeholders work together to address inequities, they acknowledge that educational justice for African American children is not just a moral imperative but also a crucial component of a just and equitable society. By removing the barriers that have historically hindered the educational progress of African American students, stakeholders help pave the way for a more inclusive and fair educational system.

By confronting and rectifying these inequities, the educational system can become more just, ensuring that African American children have the same opportunities to succeed as their peers. This not only benefits the students themselves but also contributes to a more equitable and just society overall.

Policy and Funding Reforms

In pursuit of educational justice for African American children, policy and funding reforms are critical in dismantling long-standing inequities. Educational justice requires policy changes that ensure equitable funding for schools serving African American communities. It also involves advocating for policies that support culturally relevant pedagogy, reduce disparities in disciplinary practices, and promote hiring a diverse teaching workforce that reflects the student population. Local, state, and federal policymakers can enact legislation and allocate funding that addresses systemic inequities in education. By prioritizing policies that close the opportunity gap, support underfunded schools, and promote diverse and inclusive curricula, policymakers can create the conditions necessary for educational justice. Addressing these challenges requires a deliberate effort to reevaluate and reshape existing policies and funding structures perpetuating these inequities.

Policy improvements are crucial for guaranteeing that all students, regardless of their racial or socioeconomic status, receive high-quality education. This involves reviewing regulations that regulate curriculum requirements, disciplinary measures, and teacher allocations. Historically, previous regulations were influenced by racial prejudices and adversely affected African American children. This encourages school segregation, inequitable disciplinary measures, and restricted student achievement. Reforming educational policies can cultivate an environment that promotes equity and inclusion. This will finally promote educational equity for African American children.

Funding improvements rectify the financial inequities between urban schools and their wealthy counterparts. Current financing relies on property taxes, leading to substantial resource deficiencies. This results in schools serving African American neighborhoods being inadequately supported and lacking resources. The restricted budget is evident in outdated school facilities and equipment, increased class numbers, less academically supported extracurricular activities, and restricted access to technology and educational resources. When federal, state, and local governments revise funding formulas, they must guarantee the equitable allocation of resources and furnish African American children with the essential tools for academic achievement.

The impact of policy and financial improvements on educational equity is significant. The modifications would facilitate the establishment of a more just and equitable educational environment, eliminating the academic marginalization of African American children. Schools may execute targeted interventions, ensure access to high-quality support, and cultivate an environment that fosters the potential of African American children. achieving educational equity for African American children is both a moral obligation and a societal requirement. When policy and funding are aligned with principles of justice and equity, it enables a generation of African American children to realize their full potential.

Redefining Academic Success

When society redefines educational success for African American children, it involves reinventing achievement as a means to educational equity. This approach transitions from a narrow emphasis on enhancing standardized test results in urban schools to a comprehensive approach to student achievement. It should encompass cultural identification, social-emotional growth, and community involvement. This can enable African American children to flourish in their individuality. Educators and stakeholders are redefining academic success by recognizing the students' unique cultural backgrounds and the varied talents they contribute to the classroom. This setting emphasizes the student's contribution to the classroom and society. Their success is not assessed by conventional standards.

Educational justice arises from a redefinition of academic performance. Students may view themselves as capable and significant participants in the learning process. Success entails fostering the development of African American children by providing them with resources and assistance. When educational achievement is redefined, African American children are no longer compelled to conform to a system that was not constructed for their benefit. Rather, it mirrors, promotes, and honors their potential and identities.

Moreover, educational achievement recognizes that genuine justice surpasses equality and pursues equity. Rethinking educational achievement is imperative for African American children. It promises to cultivate a future in which the educational system nurtures the potential of every child. This enables African American children to achieve brilliance according to their standards and contribute to society. This removes underlying differences in education and fosters a more equitable and inclusive future for African American children.

Ultimately, communities are enabled to assist African American children in seeing themselves as valued members of society. They receive assistance from a network of adults and peers who recognize their potential and are dedicated to their achievement. Utilizing community empowerment to achieve educational justice enhances capacity and fosters transformation. This establishes the foundation for a fair and equal educational system.

Educational Justice is Our Only Option

Educational justice is the only viable option to ensure that African American children have the opportunities, resources, and support needed to thrive. Traditional approaches to education have failed African American children with historical and systemic inequities. However, the current educational system focuses on equality but does not account for racial exclusions, economic disparities, underfunded schools, biased curriculum, and a lack of culturally responsive teaching. This created an educational environment where African American students are disproportionately impacted.

Educational justice acknowledges societal demands for solutions that go beyond equal treatment for African American children. It redefines academic success for children by affirming their identities, valuing their voices, and realizing the potential of African American children. It eliminates the one-size-fits-all methodology that is often used in the classroom. Justice cultivates African American children's sense of self and resilience and ultimately dismantles the inequities they face.

When obtaining educational justice, there is a need to confront the biases and barriers that undermine the education of African American children. It is moral and imperative that educational justice is the only option for this group of children. Embracing educational justice means committing to a vision of education that honors every child's worth and paves the way to a just and equitable future for all.

As we continue to transition from the different phases of education, I hope we can quickly arrive at a place of justice. In Figure 5, we can look at this visual and understand the true meaning of educational justice.

Figure 4: Inequality, Eq

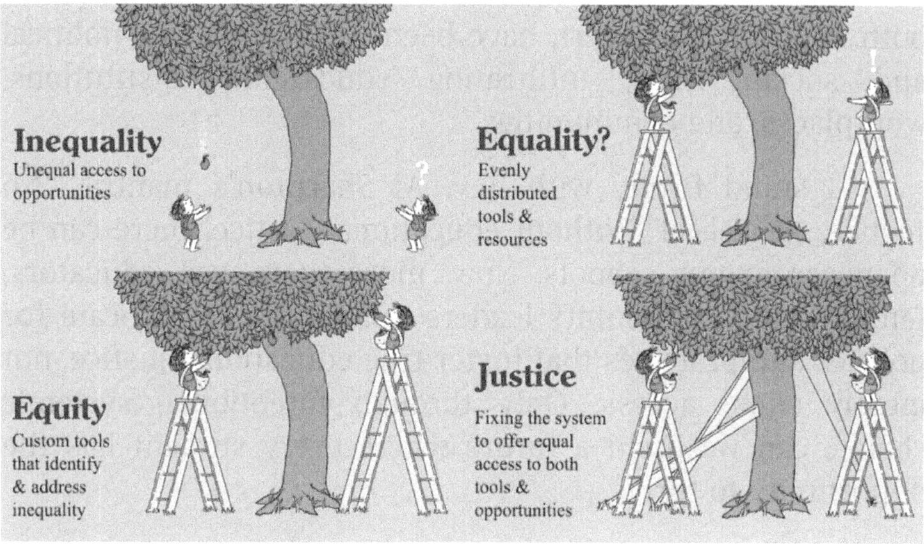

Image Credit: Tony Ruth for Design for Tech.

The inequality in schooling exclusively advantaged a specific people. They gained access to opportunities formerly restricted to African Americans. As seen in Figure 5. Numerous opportunities exist, although they are allocated to a select few. Consequently, educational equality indicates that all students receive same accommodations. A single group possesses an edge due to greater access to opportunities, while the other minority remains unable to capitalize on these prospects. Subsequently, there exists equity. Every group is provided with the necessary resources for success; yet, the marginalized group receives fewer opportunities. Justice has now been achieved. It guarantees equitable conditions for all participants. Each group is provided with necessary resources, and ample opportunities are afforded to all. That exemplifies educational equity!

In 2024, the path toward educational justice is within reach, but our society remains divided. Both implicit and explicit biases pervade our daily lives, shaping opportunities in every setting, including schools. These microaggressions, both nuanced and overt, have been woven into our political and social fabric, infiltrating educational institutions, workplaces, and communities.

I stand firmly with Rev. Al Sharpton's mantra, "No Justice, No Peace!" Without educational justice, there can be no peace in our schools. Now, more than ever, educators, families, and community leaders must actively advocate for policies and practices that foster true educational justice, not merely equal access. Only through intentional, systemic change can we build a future where every student has the opportunity to thrive.

APPENDIX

Aguilar, E. (2020). Coaching for equity. Jossey-Bass.

Ainscow, M. (2012). Moving knowledge around: Strategies for fostering equity within educational systems. Journal of Educational Change, 13(3), 289–310. https://doi.org/10.1007/s10833-012-9182-5

Almy, S., & Theokas, C. (2010). Not prepared for class: High-poverty schools continue to have fewer in-field teachers. The Education Trust. https://edtrust.org/wp-content/uploads/2013/10/Not-Prepared-for-Class.pdf

Anderson, S. G., & Olivier, D. F. (2022). A quantitative study of schools as learning organizations: An examination of professional learning communities, teacher self-efficacy, and collective efficacy. Research Issues in Contemporary Education, 7(1), 26–51. https://files.eric.ed.gov/fulltext/EJ1344350.pdf

Ashford-Hanserd, S., Springer, S. B., Hayton, M.-P., & Williams, K. E. (2020). Shadows of Plessy v. Ferguson: The dichotomy of progress toward educational equity since 1954. The Journal of Negro Education, 89(4), 410–422.

Baldwin, J. (1988). The fire next time. Laurel/Dell. (Original work published 1963).

Banks, J. (2005). African American College Students' Perceptions of Their High School Literacy Preparation. Journal of College Reading and Learning, 35(2), 22–37. https://doi-org.marymountuniv.idm.oclc.org/https://www.crla.net/journal.htm

Barnes, R. S. (2021). Transforming school-wide professional development using culturally relevant pedagogy to engage Black boys in literacy (Publication No. 28656347) [Doctoral dissertation, Fordham University]. ProQuest Dissertations and Theses Global.

Barnett, S., Carolan, M., & Johns, D. (2013). Equity and excellence: African-American children's access to quality preschool. Center on Enhancing Early Learning Outcomes and National Institute for Early Education Research. http://ceelo.org/wp-content/uploads/2017/05/EquityExcellenceAfrican-AmericanChildren.pdf

Bayar, A., & Karaduman, H. A. (2021). The effects of school culture on students academic achievement. International Journal of Education, 9(3), 99–109. https://doi.org/10.34293/education.v9i3.3885

Berry, K. N. (2023). Exploring the Experiences of Black, Low-Income Parents' Access to Quality Early Childhood Education Programs (ECE) (Order No. 31240533). Available from ProQuest Dissertations & Theses Global. (3046293287). https://marymountuniv.idm.oclc.org/login?url=https://www.proquest.com/dissertations-theses/exploring-experiences-black-low-income-parents/docview/3046293287/se-2

Bingham, G. E., Phelps, C., & Dean, M. P. (2023). Examining the Preschool to First-Grade Literacy and Language Outcomes of Black Children Experiencing a High-Quality Early Childhood Program. Elementary School Journal, 123(3), 367–395. https://doi-org.marymountuniv.idm.oclc.org/10.1086/723372

Bruce, C. D., Esmonde, I., Ross, J., Dookie, L., & Beatty, R. (2010). The effects of sustained classroom-embedded teacher professional learning on teacher efficacy and related student achievement. Teaching and Teacher Education, 26(8), 1598-1608. https://doi.org/10.1016/j.tate.2010.06.011

Chapman, T. K., & Hobbel, N. (2006). Routing the Pipeline: The Structural Dilemmas of Urban Education. Journal of Urban Learning, Teaching, and Research, 2, 116-129.

Chin, M. J., Quinn, D. M., Dhaliwal, T. K., & Lovison, V. S. (2020). Bias in the air: A nationwide exploration of teachers' implicit racial attitudes, aggregate bias, and student outcomes. Educational Researcher, 49(8), 566-578. https://doi.org/10.3102/0013189X20937240

Chism, D. (2022). Leading your school toward equity: A practical framework for walking the talk. ASCD.

Chu, Y. (2019). What are they talking about when they talk about equity? A content analysis of equity principles and provisions in state Every Student Succeeds Act plans. Education Policy Analysis Archives, 27, Article 158. https://doi.org/10.14507/epaa.27.4558

City, E. A., Elmore, R. F., Fiarman, S. E., & Teitel, L. (2009). Instructional rounds in education: A network approach to improving teaching and learning. Harvard Education Publishing Group.

Colby, I. C. (1985). The Freedmen's Bureau: From Social Welfare to Segregation. Phylon (1960-), 46(3), 219-230. https://doi.org/10.2307/274830

Colgren, C., & Sappington, N. E. (2015). Closing the achievement gap means transformation. *Education Leadership Review of Doctoral Research, 2*(1), 24-33. https://files.eric.ed.gov/fulltext/EJ1105741.pdf

Cook, C. M., Faulkner, S. A., & Howell, P. B. (2016). The developmentally responsive middle school: Meeting the needs of all students. Middle School Journal, 47(5), 3-13. https://doi.org/10.1080/00940771.2016.1226645

Cramer, E., Little, M. E., & McHatton, P. A. (2018). Equity, equality, and standardization: Expanding the conversations. Education and Urban Society, 50(5), 483-501. https://doi.org/10.1177/0013124517713249

Dack, H., Chiles, E., Kathman, L., Poessnecker, A., & Strohl, E. (2022). The key to equitable differentiation. Middle School Journal, 53(5), 15-32. https://doi.org/10.1080/00940771.2022.2119756

Darling-Hammond, L. (2006). Securing the right to learn: Policy and practice for powerful teaching and learning. Educational Researcher, 35(7), 13-24. https://doi.org/10.3102/0013189X035007013

Datnow, A., & Park, V. (2018). Opening or closing doors for students? Equity and data use in schools. Journal of Educational Change, 19(2), 131-152. https://doi.org/10.1007/s10833-018-9323-6

DeCuir, J. T., & Dixson, A. D. (2004). "So when it comes out, they aren't that surprised that it is there": Using critical race theory as a tool of analysis of race and racism in education. Educational Researcher, 33(5), 26-31. https://doi.org/10.3102/0013189X033005026

Delale-O'Connor, L. A., Alvarez, A. J., Murray, I. E., & Milner, H. R., IV. (2017). Self-Efficacy Beliefs, Classroom Management, and the Cradle-to-Prison Pipeline. Theory Into Practice, 56(3), 178–186. https://doi-org.marymountuniv.idm.oclc.org/10.1080/00405841.2017.1336038

DiCicco, M., Cook, C. M., & Faulkner, S. A. (2016). Teaching in the middle grades today: Examining teachers' beliefs about middle grades teaching. Middle Grades Review, 2(3), Article 3. https://scholarworks.uvm.edu/cgi/viewcontent.cgi?article=1046&context=mgreview

Ellerbrock, C. R., Cruz, B. C., Vasquez, A., & Howes, E. V. (2016). Preparing culturally responsive teachers: Effective practices in teacher education. Action in Teacher Education, 38(3), 226–239. https://doi.org/10.1080/01626620.2016.1194780

Elmore, R. (2008). Improving the instructional core. https://www.pps.net/site/handlers/filedownload.ashx?moduleinstanceid=19185&dataid=123381&FileName=Improving_the_Instructional_Core.pdf

Evans, A. (2009). No Child Left Behind and the quest for educational equity: The role of teachers' collective sense of efficacy. Leadership and Policy in Schools, 8(1), 64–91. https://doi.org/10.1080/15700760802416081

Evans, L. M., Turner, C. R., & Allen, K. R. (2020). "Good teachers" with "good intentions": Misappropriations of culturally responsive pedagogy. Journal of Urban Learning, 15(1), 51–73. https://doi.org/10.51830/jultr.3

Filmer, A. A. (2003). African-American Vernacular English: Ethics, Ideology, and Pedagogy in the Conflict between Identity and Power. World Englishes: Journal of English as an International and Intranational Language, 22(3), 253-270.

Fisher, D., & Lapp, D. (2013). Learning to Talk Like the Test: Guiding Speaker of African American Vernacular English. Journal of Adolescent & Adult Literacy, 56(8), 634-648. http://www.jstor.org/stable/41827918

Grace, J. E., & Nelson, S. L. (2019). "Tryin" to Survive': Black Male Students' Understandings of the Role of Race and Racism in the School-to-Prison Pipeline. Leadership and Policy in Schools, 18(4), 664-680. https://doi-org.marymountuniv.idm.oclc.org/10.1080/15700763.2018.1513154

Gregory, A., Skiba, R. J., & Noguera, P. A. (2010). The achievement gap and the discipline gap: Two sides of the same coin? Educational Researcher, 39(1), 59-68. https://doi.org/10.3102/0013189X09357621

Harris, Y. R., & Schroeder, V. M. (2013). Language Deficits or Differences: What We Know about African American Vernacular English in the 21st Century. International Education Studies, 6(4), 194-204.

Hedrick, K. A. (2012). Differentiation: A strategic response to student needs. The School Administrator, 78(4), 31-36.

Howard, T. C. (2008). Who really cares? The disenfranchisement of African American males in PreK-12 schools: A critical race theory perspective. Teachers College Record, 10(5), 954-985. https://doi.org/10.1177/016146810811000507

Iruka, I. U. (2022). Delivering on the Promise of Early Childhood Education for Black Children: An Equity Strategy. New Directions for Child and Adolescent Development, 183–184, 27–45. https://doi-org.marymountuniv.idm.oclc.org/10.1002/cad.20483

Jacobs, L., Brown, K., Washington, K., OConnor, J., & Lundin, M. (2022). Disrupting the School to Prison Pipeline: Using Culturally Responsive Classroom Practices to Support Black Students. School Leadership Review, 16(2).

Jarrett, R. L., & Coba-Rodriguez, S. (2018). How African American mothers from urban, low-income backgrounds support their children's kindergarten transition: Qualitative findings. Early Childhood Education Journal, 46(4), 435–444. https://doi.org/10.1007/s10643-017-0868-4

Johnson, K. P., Graves, S. L., Jones, M. A., Phillips, S., & Jacobs, M. (2023). Understanding African American Vernacular English and Reading Achievement: Implications for the Science of Reading. School Psychology, 38(1), 7–14. https://doi-org.marymountuniv.idm.oclc.org/10.1037/spq0000516

Kanevsky, L. (2011). Deferential differentiation. Gifted Child Quarterly, 55(4), 279–299. https://doi.org/10.1177/0016986211422098

Kendi, I. X. (2017). Stamped from the beginning: The definitive history of racist ideas in America. Bold Type Books.
Ladson-Billings, G. (2009). The dream-keepers: Successful teachers of African American children (2nd ed.). Jossey-Bass.

Lareau, A. (2011). Unequal childhoods: class, race, and family life (2nd ed.). University of California Press.

Lawrence, C., III. (2005). Forbidden conversations: On race, privacy, and community (A continuing conversation with John Ely on racism and democracy). Yale Law School. https://digitalcommons.law.yale.edu/cgi/viewcontent.cgi?article=4953&context=ylj

Lazaro, V. L. (2006). Factors that influence the achievement of economically disadvantaged students in a large, urban Texas school district: A critical race analysis of equitable academic success (Publication No. 3215925) [Doctoral dissertation, The University of Texas at Austin]. ProQuest Dissertations and Theses Global.

Lewis, C. (2012). Oppositional culture and educational opportunity. Theory and Research in Education, 10(2), 131-154. https://doi.org/10.1177/1477878512448131

Linton, C. (2011). Equity 101--The equity framework. Corwin Press.

Lorenzetti, N., & Johnson, H. (2022). It starts in the classroom: The relationship between teacher education students' implicit racial biases and classroom disciplinary decisions. Journal of Research in Education, 31(1), 69-91. https://files.eric.ed.gov/fulltext/EJ1368471.pdf

Lotan, R. (2006). Teaching teachers to build equitable classrooms. Theory Into Practice, 45(1), 32-39. https://doi.org/10.1207/s15430421tip4501_5

Mesa, M. P., Roehrig, A., Funari, C., Durtschi, S., Ha, C., Rawls, E., & Davis, C. (2021). Young African American Scholars Make Reading Gains at Literacy-Focused, Culturally Relevant Summer Camp That Combats Summer Reading Loss. Grantee Submission, 59(1), 252–267. https://doi-org.marymountuniv.idm.oclc.org/https://feraonline.org/article/1-young-african-american-scholars-make-reading-gains-at-literacy-focused-culturally-relevant-summer-camp-that-combats-summer-reading-loss/

Muhammad, G. E., Dunmeyer, A., Starks, F. D., & Sealey Ruiz, Y. (2020). Historical voices for contemporary times: Learning from Black women educational theorists to redesign teaching and teacher education. Theory Into Practice, 59(4), 419–428. https://doi.org/10.1080/00405841.2020.1773185

Nieto, S. (2005). Public education in the twentieth century and beyond: High hopes, broken promises, and an uncertain future. Harvard Educational Review, 75(1), 43–64. https://doi.org/10.17763/haer.75.1.31r4357517211566

O'Keeffe, L., Paige, K., & Osborne, S. (2019). Getting started: Exploring pre-service teachers' confidence and knowledge of culturally responsive pedagogy in teaching mathematics and science. Asia-Pacific Journal of Teacher Education, 47(2), 152–175. https://doi.org/10.1080/1359866X.2018.1531386

Perkins, J. H., & Cooter, R. B., Jr. (2005). Evidence-based literacy education and the African American child. The Reading Teacher, 59(2), 194–198. https://doi.org/10.1598/RT.59.2.9

Rashid, H. M. (2009). From Brilliant Baby to Child Placed at Risk: The Perilous Path of African American Boys in Early Childhood Education. Journal of Negro Education, 78(3), 347–358. https://doi-org.marymountuniv.idm.oclc.org/https://www.journalnegroed.org/recentissues.htm

Ready, D. D., & Chu, E. M. (2015). Sociodemographic inequality in early literacy development: The role of teacher perceptual accuracy. Early Education and Development, 26(7), 970–987. https://doi.org/10.1080/10409289.2015.1004516

Rucker, W. C., & Jubilee, S. K. (2007). From Black Nadir to Brown v. Board: Education and Empowerment in Black Georgian Communities - 1865 to 1954. Negro Educational Review, The, 58(3-4), 151–168. https://doi-org.marymountuniv.idm.oclc.org/https://oma.osu.edu/vice_provost/ner/index.html

Sandoval, J. M., Challoo, L. B., & Kupczynski, L. (2011). The relationship between teachers' collective efficacy and student achievement at economically disadvantaged middle school campuses. Journal on Educational Psychology, 5(1), 9–23. https://doi.org/10.26634/jpsy.5.1.1494

Schaeffer, K. (2021, December 10). America's public school teachers are far less racially and ethnically diverse than their students. Pew Research Center. https://www.pewresearch.org/short-reads/2021/12/10/americas-public-school-teachers-are-far-less-racially-and-ethnically-diverse-than-their-students/ - :~:text=White teachers, on the other

Stembridge, A. (2020). Culturally responsive education in the classroom: An equity framework for pedagogy. Routledge.

Straus, L. P. (2011). Adolescent reading engagement: Predictors of eighth grade reading achievement on the 2007 NAEP with an examination of gender and ethnicity differences (Publication No. 3466685) [Doctoral dissertation, The Claremont Graduate University]. ProQuest Dissertations and Theses Global.

Snow, P. C. (2019). Speech-Language Pathology and the Youth Offender: Epidemiological Overview and Roadmap for Future Speech-Language Pathology Research and Scope of Practice. Language, Speech, and Hearing Services in Schools, 50(2), 324–339. https://doi-org.marymountuniv.idm.oclc.org/10.1044/2018_LSHSS-CCJS-18-0027

Thompson, D. A. (2022). K-12 principals' perceptions regarding culturally responsive school leadership self-efficacy: Main effect and interactions of race, gender, and school level (Publication No. 29391380) [Doctoral dissertation, Regent University]. ProQuest Dissertations and Theses Global.

Tomlinson, C. A. (1999). Mapping a route toward differentiated instruction. Educational Leadership, 57(1), 12–16. https://files.ascd.org/staticfiles/ascd/pdf/journals/ed_lead/el199909_tomlinson.pdf

Williams, M. J. (2023). Teacher perceptions of differentiated instruction in a standards-based grading middle school. Educational Research: Theory and Practice, 34(1), 129–150. https://www.nrmera.org/wp-content/uploads/2023/03/V34-1_9-Williams-Teacher-Perceptions-of-Differentiated-Instruction.pdf

Warikoo, N., Sinclair, S., Fei, J., & Jacoby-Senghor, D. (2016). Examining racial bias in education: A new approach. Educational Researcher, 45(9), 508–514. https://doi.org/10.3102/0013189X16683408

Yang, J. L., Anyon, Y., Pauline, M., Wiley, K. E., Cash, D., Downing, B. J., Greer, E., Kelty, E., Morgan, T. L., & Pisciotta, L. (2018). "We Have to Educate Every Single Student, Not Just the Ones That Look Like Us": Support Service Providers' Beliefs about the Root Causes of the School-to-Prison Pipeline for Youth of Color. Equity & Excellence in Education, 51(3–4), 316–331. https://doi.org.marymountuniv.idm.oclc.org/10.1080/1066 5684.2018.1539358

ABOUT THE AUTHOR

Dr. Yashima L. Thomas-Jones, a native of New Jersey, is the daughter of Mrs. Roslyn and the late Victor Thomas. She resides in Union, New Jersey, with her husband, Jeffrey Jones, and is the proud sister of Haneefah Thomas. Dr. Yashima adores her nieces Eniyah, Laila, and nephew Haneef, and she is proud to be the godmother of Skylar, Mya-Ashilee, Nasir, Dontaye, and Amauri.

Dr. Yashima graduated with a BA in psychology from New Jersey City University in 1997. She then obtained a Master of Arts in Special Education in 2011. Dr. Jones furthered her education and completed a second master's in urban education leadership in 2015. In 2021, Dr. Yashima enrolled in the doctoral program at Marymount University. She successfully graduated in May 2024 with her doctorate in education.

After completing her undergraduate degree, she started her career working with the Occupational Center of Orange as an employment counselor for adults with disabilities. Before pursuing her career in education, she worked for Hudson County Correctional Facility and the Division of Youth and Family Services. In 2004, God guided her to transition into education because he had a greater purpose in helping impact the lives of children.

Dr. Yashima began teaching at Liberty Academy Charter School in Jersey City, New Jersey in 2004. She transitioned to the Elizabeth Public School system as a special education teacher in 2007. Dr. Yashima was an in-class support special education teacher until 2018 when she became a middle school learning language disabilities teacher. She has dedicated 20 years to teaching in urban schools. Throughout this time, Dr. Yashima L. Thomas-Jones has been actively involved in the school community, continuously striving to improve student learning outcomes through equitable teaching practices. With a daily goal to empower students to be their best selves, Dr. Yashima works diligently to provide a supportive and inclusive learning environment.

Furthermore, Dr. Yashima's extensive experience in early intervention, assisting parents in helping their children meet early development milestones, is a testament to her expertise in child development. This role has allowed her to significantly impact children's foundational growth and development, ensuring they are well-prepared for their educational journey.

Dr. Yashima's passion and love for preparing students for their future extend beyond the classroom. In 2008, in collaboration with her church and several other organizations, she began an annual end-of-summer distribution of bookbags, uniforms, school supplies, and gift cards to students in the community. She stands firm on Isaiah 61:1-3, where God commands that we instruct to preach good tiding, heal the brokenhearted, proclaim liberty to the captives, open prison doors to those who are bound, comfort those who mourn, give beauty for ashes, oil of joy, and the garment of praise for the spirit of heaviness.

Dr. Yashima's unwavering dedication to teaching and students' success, with God's help, has made a lasting difference in the lives of countless students and their families. Her belief that her students are destined for greatness is a source of optimism for the future of education.

From the Publisher

GREAT BOOKS

ARE EVEN BETTER WHEN THEY'RE SHARED!

HELP OTHER READERS FIND THIS ONE:

- Post reviews at your favorite online booksellers

- Post a picture on your social media accounts and share why you enjoyed it

- Send a note to a friend or colleague who would also love it-or better yet, gift them a copy!

Thanks for reading!

Made in the USA
Middletown, DE
19 November 2024

64692488R00096